"This is a book whose message is long overdue, both for the general public and the academic community ... After years of reading 'one side' of the story, I strongly felt there was 'this story' saved somewhere and yet to be told."

—Arthur Einhorn, ethnohistorian

"What results from reading this fine book is a totally different understanding of Pocahontas's life. The authors have eminent qualifications to present in print 'the other side of the story.' Their book deserves to be studied carefully and to hold a place on your bookshelf alongside the others by Helen C. Rountree, Frances Mossiker, and Camilla Townsend. *The True Story of Pocahontas* is a must-read for anyone interested in the full story of the epic of Jamestown and its participants."

—Robert Shultis, *The Virginia Gazette*

"This side of history, the knowledge of Pochahontas from her own people, is a profound story long overdue. This book affords important insights into ecological harmony and living with love for one another in peace."

—Jeffrey Hopkins, professor emeritus of Tibetan studies, University of Virginia

"*The True Story of Pocahontas* stands out as one of the greatest true stories of family love, dedication, and tragedy."

—*Indian Country Today*

"The book provides an incredible look inside the Mattaponi Indians and the Powhatan Nation and also provides insights into contact with Spanish explorers long before the English arrived in Virginia."

—Bill Archer, *Bluefield Daily Telegraph*

"Their history has been held secret since the arrival of the colonists. Until now, the words shared in this book were known by only a cherished few."

—Kerry Day, *Fifty Plus*

The True Story of Pocahontas

THE OTHER SIDE OF HISTORY

The True Story of Pocahontas

THE OTHER SIDE OF HISTORY

From the Sacred History of the Mattaponi Reservation People

Dr. Linwood "Little Bear" Custalow and Angela L. Daniel "Silver Star"

Fulcrum Publishing
Wheat Ridge, Colorado

Library of Congress Cataloging-in-Publication Data
Custalow, Linwood.
  The true story of Pocahontas : the other side of history / Linwood
"Little Bear" Custalow and Angela L. Daniel.
    p. cm.
  Includes bibliographical references.
  ISBN-13: 978-1-55591-632-9 (pbk. : alk. paper)
  ISBN-10: 1-55591-632-5
  1. Pocahontas, d. 1617. 2. Powhatan women--Biography. 3. Powhatan
Indians--Social life and customs. I. Daniel, Angela L. II. Title.
  E99.P85P62 2007
  975.5'01092--dc22
                            2006033719

Printed in the United States of America
20 19 18 17 16 15 14 13 12 11

The authors gratefully acknowledge the following people for granting permission to reprint their photographs: the Virginia Historical Society, Richmond; the Borough Council of King's Lynn and West Norfolk; Mattaponi Chief Carl "Lone Eagle" Custalow; Deborah "White Dove" Custalow Porreco; Shirley "Little Dove" Custalow McGowan; Kathryn Cannada and sons; Justin Kyle Whitman; Edith "White Feather" Custalow Kuhns; and Rachel "Talking Moon" McGowan. A special thank-you to Bill Faust II for the use of his photograph of the Custalow family and Louise Krafft for her photograph of Rachel "Talking Moon" McGowan.

Cover and interior design: Jack Lenzo
Cover image: © Index Open/Fogstock LLC

Fulcrum Publishing
3970 Youngfield Street
Wheat Ridge, Colorado 80033
800-992-2908 • 303-277-1623
www.fulcrumbooks.com

Dedicated to

Chief Daniel Webster "Little Eagle" Custalow
November 14, 1912, to March 21, 2003
Chief of the Mattaponi tribe

Indians were friendly people. They were loving people. An Indian would give you the last thing he had if you treated him halfway right. I heard my grandfather say so.

—Chief Daniel Webster "Little Eagle" Custalow

Chief Custalow is remembered for his huge heart, his capacity for giving, and his captivating presence. "He was like a magnet. People would line up to talk to him," said one of his four sons, Mattaponi Chief Carl "Lone Eagle" Custalow. "He wasn't the most educated man, but people were educated by him and consoled by him. It's like he was a doctor, a lawyer, and an Indian chief."

And to
Donald "Bright Path" Kuhns

July 12, 1955, to November 28, 1999
Warrior, teacher, Powhatan artisan, and the first grandson of
the late Daniel Webster "Little Eagle" Custalow

**My grandfather told me to 'spread the word' about our ancestry.
There is a pride in teaching our heritage.**

—Donald "Bright Path" Kuhns

As a young child, Donald was always playing in the woods. He
was given the name Wahtahhoch, which means "bright path."

I could always find my way home.

—Donald "Bright Path" Kuhns

"Bright Path" did so much to make sure
our people were not forgotten.

Only from truthful history can true history be learned.
Only by true history can we learn from our mistakes.
Only by learning from our mistakes can we create a
better life for all mankind. We can only learn from the
real history; many don't see the real history!

—Dr. Linwood "Little Bear" Custalow

Prayer to the Great Spirit Ahone

Ahone,
Ahone,
Ahone,
Ahone,
Aho!
Oh, Good and Great Spirit,*

you who are all knowledgeable,
all wise, and all understanding,
grant me your wisdom, knowledge,
and understanding to present the full
Mattaponi tribal history in conjunction
with written history and research in truth
that it may not cast blame or be offensive,
but in a way that it may be enlightening
to all who read this book.

May the true history of the past acknowledge
mistakes, aggressions, deceits, prejudices, wrongful intents, greed, and
injustices.
May we present our history in love, withholding nothing,
that we may see the past as a helpful tool to make the changes that we
need in order
to walk together in harmony and in love and justice.
Let us borrow each other's moccasins so that we may see each other's
point of view.
Let us walk in the present and not in the past
that we may make this day and all of our future days a better place for
your creation.
May you see us as pleasing from your great moccasins.

Aho!

—Dr. Linwood "Little Bear" Custalow,

eldest son of the late Chief Daniel Webster "Little Eagle" Custalow

---

* It is important to remember to call on Ahone, the Good and Great Spirit. One must call to the four winds, or four directions. Ahone is not omnipresent in the concept of the Powhatan. Our ancestors could not conceive of God being everywhere at the same time or present in all periods of time at once. It was a concept they had not grasped.

Statue, *Indian Princess—Pocahontas* in Gloucester, Virginia, erected in 1994. It is considered to be the only authentic depiction of Pocahontas as a youth. Extensive research was conducted for authenticity by Powhatan descendant Deborah "White Dove" Custalow Porreco and the statue's sculptor, Adolf Sehring. Photograph by Angela L. Daniel "Silver Star"

Contents

Part Two

Tsenacomoca 1607–1613

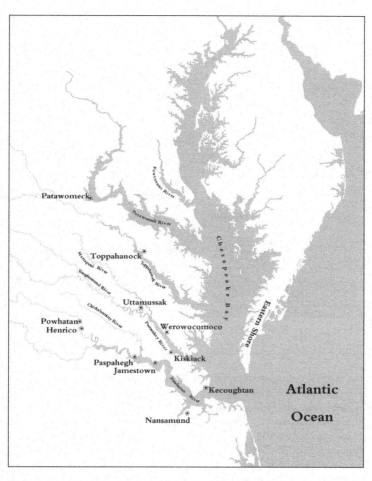

Our land was called Tsenacamoca in the Powhatan language. The English called it Virginia Britannia or Virginia. The map shows the approximate location of some of the prominent Powhatan villages and English-colonist settlements from 1607 to 1613.

Present-Day Virginia

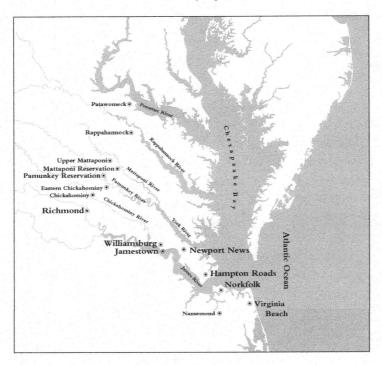

The Powhatan chiefdom once held an alliance of thirty-two-plus tribes. Today, there are only eight state-recognized tribes in Virginia, five of which were part of the Powhatan chiefdom during the late seventeenth century: Pamunkey, Mattaponi, Nansemond (Nansamund), Rappahannock, and Chickahominy. The current-day Eastern Chickahominy tribe spilt off from the Chickahominy and Pamunkey tribes. The Upper Mattaponi tribe is a newly formed tribe, organized in the 1980s. None of the Virginia tribes have been granted federal recognition, and some have not yet received state recognition, such as the Powhatan Patawomeck (Potowomac) tribe. Only the Pamunkey and the Mattaponi tribes have been able to retain reservation land; they have also maintained an unbroken peace treaty with the Commonwealth of Virginia since 1646. This map shows the approximate location of eight remaining eastern Virginia tribes that were related to the Powhatan chiefdom.*

* For an overview of contemporary Virginia Indians, see *We're Still Here: Contemporary Virginia Indians Tell Their Stories* by Sandra F. Waugaman and Danielle Moretti-Lanholtz, PhD (Richmond, VA: Palari Publishing, 2000).

Mattaponi Chief Carl "Lone Eagle" Custalow. Photograph by Angela L. Daniel "Silver Star"

Letter from Mattaponi Chief Carl "Lone Eagle" Custalow

I don't see a time when this history was more needed for my people than now. Our oral history has been kept hidden for so long, it's dying. People have not looked through our cultural lens at history. It's time to look at the other side of history, the sacred history of the Mattaponi.

I write this letter while watching the rain fall outside my home on the reservation. I look at the Mattaponi River below, and I see things not seen by most people. I live on the river and my people live here. We are the people of the river. The river and the reservation are our life. Interwoven with our daily lives, the river has always been a source of deep honor and self-preservation.

Life for our ancestors was a harsh struggle. Our land and food sources were taken from us. Later, laws were passed severely limiting our rights, banishing us from public schools. We were forced to live outside mainstream activities and culture. During the 1940s, '50s, and all the many moons back to the first English settlement at Jamestown, we would not have considered telling the true story of Pocahontas. Even my father knew he could not tell our history: people were not open to hearing it. Deeply embedded, our experiences, our memories, and our dreams have lain secret for almost 400 years.

From the earliest period in Mattaponi history, we were able to thrive, develop, and later survive the English colonists' arrival and settlement of our land because of the Mattaponi River. Today, the Mattaponi River, with its vast acres of wetlands and endangered fish and wildlife, is threatened by a proposed dam, the King William Reservoir dam. Our very survival is once again threatened: if the river is destroyed, we have nowhere else to go. We have no alternative but to fight the construction of this proposed dam.

Today, we are not alone. Others have stepped forward to support us in our fight to save the river. For the first time, through mutual respect, people have become emotionally, if not physically, invested in our survival. People want to hear the truth. They are open to it. It is time to tell our oral history. *The True Story of Pocahontas* will help everyone gain a sense of our cultural history, learn lessons not taught in school, and discover the deep historical connections between tribes as well as with other communities. As you read this book, look at us through our eyes.

Reading my brother's words, sensing the excitement in his voice, the way he describes our tribe's past with such spirit and courage, his humility about his own position as recorder and protector of our history, and even his own physical condition assure me that now is the time to tell the other side of history, the Mattaponi side. No one knows our history better than Lin "Little Bear." His passion for learning our oral history has brought unusual insights to it. Lin "Little Bear" has stayed the course when many would have faltered. Angela "Silver Star" has made it possible for all things once safeguarded in Lin's mind and heart to be recorded and preserved for future generations. For this, I will be forever grateful.

This small book honors not only Pocahontas, but all Mattaponi.

With warm regards,

I am,

Mattaponi Chief Carl "Lone Eagle" Custalow

Who We Are

Dr. Linwood "Little Bear" Custalow's Teachers of the Mattaponi Sacred Oral History

Mattaponi Chief George "Thunder Cloud" F. Custalow Sr., circa 1910.

Travel in all four directions as the four winds blow and teach the history of our people.

—Dr. Linwood "Little Bear" Custalow's grandfather Mattaponi Chief George "Thunder Cloud" F. Custalow Sr. (1865–1949)

Dr. Linwood "Little Bear" Custalow's uncle, Mattaponi Chief Otha T. (O. T.) "Hos-ki-no-wa-na-ha" Custalow (1898–1969).

The surviving Powhatan priests decided that the maintenance of Powhatan tribal history was important because history tell us who we are.

—Dr. Linwood "Little Bear" Custalow

Dr. Linwood "Little Bear" Custalow's father, Mattaponi Chief Daniel Webster "Little Eagle" Custalow (1912–2003).

Dr. Linwood "Little Bear" Custalow's Family Members Who Carry Aspects of Mattaponi Sacred Oral History

Standing on the banks of the Mattaponi River, the late Mattaponi Chief Webster "Little Eagle" Custalow is flanked by two of his daughters, (left) Shirley "Little Dove" Custalow McGowan and (right) Deborah "White Dove" Custalow Porreco, and (far right) by his oldest son, Dr. Linwood "Little Bear" Custalow.

Deborah "White Dove" has represented Pocahontas in various historical reenactments and documentaries. Photograph by Bill Faust II

Edith "White Feather" Custalow Kuhns, a daughter of the late Mattaponi Chief Webster "Little Eagle" Custalow, participates in the Mattaponi annual powwow of 2006. Dr. Linwood "Little Bear" Custalow, Shirley "Little Dove" Custalow McGowan, and Edith "White Feather" are passing the Powhatan oral history on to future generations. Photograph by Angela L. Daniel "Silver Star"

Wingapo na-tap-a-wah.
Mattaponi a-nee-ah-nee-o-wah.
"Welcome, my good friend. I am from the Mattaponi."
[ma-tə-pō-nē]

The Powhatan history of Pocahontas has been orally passed down from generation to generation. You have not read this story before; this is the first written history of Pocahontas by her own people. It is vastly different from the history you have been taught from school, novels, and movies.

Because the Powhatan people did not have a written language, our knowledge, religious and secular, was kept in the hearts and minds of a chosen few, the priests, or *quiakros* [kē-ā-krōs], who dedicated their lives to learning. There were many *quiakros* in our society—at least one or more in each tribe—who maintained, preserved, and imparted knowledge, preserving the history of the particular tribe in which they served. The Powhatan *quiakros* were like living libraries. The *quiakros* of the Uttamussac Temple were the highest order to serve the Powhatan nation.

Knowing how important *quiakros* were to the Powhatan society, the English sought to annihilate them. As the Powhatan society began to collapse after the war of 1644 to 1646, toward the middle of the seventeenth century the *quiakros* of the Powhatan nation elected to remain stealth under the Mattaponi tribe. The Mattaponi chief sought to conceal the remaining Powhatan *quiakros* among our people from the English. (The Pamunkey tribe was busy maintaining secular relations for the Powhatan tribes with the English.) This meant that the Mattaponi tribe had to remain clandestine until the last decade of the nineteenth century.

Of all the possible types of knowledge to maintain, history is considered the most important. Our history tells us who we are. We have passed this knowledge on through the *quiakros*, then through the chiefs, for generations. It is sacred to us.

I have spent my life learning our sacred oral history. Today, I share that responsibility by passing on the knowledge of the tribe's oral history to Angela L. Daniel "Silver Star," my coauthor. Together, we are recording the sacred oral history of the Mattaponi for future generations to know.

We invite you into our world that you might begin to know us for who we are.

—Dr. Linwood "Little Bear" Custalow,

historian of the Mattaponi Indian tribe,

Williamsburg, Virginia, 2004

The Other Side of History

"Tell the true story of Pocahontas!"

I hear this plea when I walk among Pocahontas's people. *The True Story of Pocahontas: The Other Side of History* is the story of Pocahontas as told by her own people. Buried under fame and myth, the true story of Pocahontas according to her Powhatan descendants has never been published before. It has been hidden for nearly 400 years within the Mattaponi tribe out of fear of violent retribution if it were told publicly. At the same time, it is about more than one person, Pocahontas; it is about the Powhatan people entering an era of immense changes.

The True Story of Pocahontas incorporates the sacred oral history of the Mattaponi. Maintaining this history has been a long-term tribal effort; the history is not from the insight or opinion of one person. Dr. Linwood "Little Bear" Custalow has been learning the Mattaponi sacred oral history since childhood from late chiefs of the Mattaponi tribe, including his father, Webster "Little Eagle" Custalow; his uncle Otha T. (O. T.) Custalow; and his grandfather Chief George "Thunder Cloud" F. Custalow. Those who have gone before him made it possible to pass this history on. In addition, other Mattaponi confirm Lin "Little Bear's" rendition, including Shirley "Little Dove" Custalow McGowan and Edith "White Feather" Custalow Kuhns.

Oral history/tradition does not comprise "made-up" stories. In the seventeenth century and before, history was maintained by the *quiakros* (Powhatan priests). It was passed down from generation to generation in a very strict and disciplined manner to maintain accuracy. During the starvation period of the late 1600s into the 1800s, the population of the Powhatan people, as well as the number of *quiakros*, rapidly declined. Up until the early 1900s, a *quiakro* held the position of what is called an *assistant chief* today.

The True Story of Pocahontas also provides readers with

the Powhatan interpretation of events documented in seventeenth-century English writings.

This book is an attempt by the Mattaponi to document in a written format their sacred history, which has been maintained orally for centuries. There are many benefits to a written tradition: it can reach a vast number of people, and it is also less vulnerable to being lost.

Still, there are attributes of oral traditions that are not obtainable in a written format. For example, the written word seems inadequate in capturing the spirit and emotions that poured forth from Lin "Little Bear's" telling of the sacred history of his people. In the oral tellings, people of the past, such as Pocahontas and her father, Chief Powhatan Wahunsenaca, came alive, with real emotions. It was like they were still living, in the present, within the heart of the oral historian. At times, tears would flow when the telling of historic events became horrific. There is a living connection between the oral historian and his or her ancestors.

Lin "Little Bear" appears to have a strong connection with his late father, Chief Daniel Webster "Little Eagle" Custalow. One time while we were talking, Lin "Little Bear" appeared to transform into the late Chief "Little Eagle." Lin "Little Bear" assumed the facial features and body stance of his late father. As Lin "Little Bear" repositioned himself in the chair, I sat silently, not letting on to what my eyes beheld.

Finally, I broke the silence, stating, "The purpose of history, it has been said, is to learn from history, but it does not seem as though it is put into practice very often."

Quickly, Lin "Little Bear" responded, "We can only learn from the real history. Many don't see the real history! The reason we have not learned from history is because we have not embraced the truth of what has happened."

—Angela L. Daniel "Silver Star"

College of William & Mary, Department of Anthropology,

PhD Program, Williamsburg, Virginia

How To Tell the Story?

Our concern in writing down the oral history of our people was to find a way to keep the content and sequence of events and still convey the rhythm and power of speech. We have chosen to include in this book many of the actual words and sentences as spoken by Dr. Linwood "Little Bear" Custalow, the oral historian of the Mattaponi tribe. The Mattaponi tribe of Virginia is one of the few remaining tribes of the great Powhatan nation that the English colonists encountered during their establishment of Jamestown. Along with the Pamunkey tribe, the Mattaponi tribe was one of the first six original core tribes forming the Powhatan nation. The four other core Powhatan tribes were Appamatuck, Arrohateck, Youghtanund, and Powhatan.[1] The Powhatan nation included more than thirty tribes before its collapse.[2] The Mattaponi tribe is one of the two last remaining of the six original tribes that formed the Powhatan nation, who reside on one of the only two reservations in Virginia. The other tribes that enlarged the Powhatan nation came in by alliance.

The narrative of the book is true to this oral history. Its language and structure are designed for our eyes as well as our ears. Between the more relaxed format of the spoken word and the more formalized structure of the written language that together compose this book, we hope you will be able to take this story into your heart as well as your mind.

Rachel "Talking Moon" McGowan, granddaughter of Shirley "Little Dove" Custalow McGowan, 2004. The publication of the Mattaponi oral history is to ensure that it is not lost, as many other aspects of our culture, such as our language, have been. According to our heritage, the past and the future coincide in the present. We pass the sacred knowledge to our present and future generations. Photograph by Louise Krafft

PART ONE

Teach the full Indian history. That is the problem today:
too much Indian (First American) history has been left out.

—Mattaponi tribal member

CHAPTER ONE

Pocahontas: A Favorite Child

The story of Pocahontas is first and foremost a great love story. The love that was the moving force within Pocahontas's life was the spiritual bond and filial affection between Pocahontas and her father, Chief Powhatan Wahunsenaca,[1] and the love they had for the Powhatan people. Wahunsenaca was the paramount chief of the Powhatan nation.

Pocahontas and Wahunsenaca's father-daughter rela-tion-ship was so strong that even the English colonists recognized that Pocahontas was the favorite child of the paramount chief.[2] What the English colonists did not know was why Pocahontas was held so dearly in the heart of this paramount chief. After all, Wahunsenaca had many children.

Customs were different in seventeenth-century Powha-tan culture. Being the paramount chief of the Powhatan chief-dom, called Tsenacomoca, Wahunsenaca married young maidens from each of the tribes within the alliance. The tradition was to infuse all the tribes with blood from the primary leader and to provide relational ties and obligations throughout the chiefdom to unite the tribes under one paramount leader and enlarge the Powhatan nation.

It was a great honor for a young woman to be asked by her tribe to be taken in marriage with the paramount chief. She could decline, if she so desired. Women were not forced into marriage, not even with the paramount chief. However, this was considered not only a great honor, but it provided the woman with a great deal of political and social clout. Few would have declined the opportunity. If a woman refused, the position would have been filled quickly by a woman who was agreeable to the arrangement.

These were alliance marriages—not marriages of love,

but of politics and agreement. Love marriages were more permanent. An alliance marriage was meant to seal the alliance between the Powhatan nation and the incoming tribe. It was a temporary marriage in order to infuse royal blood into the alliance tribe and to establish kinship ties. This custom was limited to the paramount chief of the Powhatan nation. After the alliance wife gave birth, she had the choice of living in Werowocomoco, the secular capital village of the Powhatan nation, or returning to her village. Due to the prestigious nature of this position in Powhatan society, the alliance wife would have had no difficulty in finding a "real" husband. Instead, she would have been highly sought after for marriage. She would have been highly esteemed.

The mother of little Pocahontas was Wahunsenaca's first wife; her name was also Pocahontas. They were married before he became the paramount chief. The mother of little Pocahontas was his wife of choice, the wife of love to Wahunsenaca. The marriages to the young maidens from the alliance tribes held more of a sense of responsibility and obligation to the welfare of Tsenacomoca, the entire chiefdom. The mother of little Pocahontas was his wife of love, not of compliance to customs; therefore, Pocahontas's mother held a special place in Wahunsenaca's heart.

Sadly, Pocahontas's mother died while giving birth to Pocahontas. Wahunsenaca was devastated. Overcome with grief, he found a spiritual connection to his lost wife in their child. Little Pocahontas was given the name Matoaka at birth. Matoaka translates as "flower between two streams." The name was most likely given to her because the Mattaponi village was located between the Mattaponi and the Pamunkey (York) Rivers. Matoaka's parents were from the Mattaponi and Pamunkey tribes—her mother was Mattaponi; her father was Pamunkey.*

---

* It is interesting that, later in life, Pocahontas became the Powhatan symbol of peace between two vastly different cultures, the Powhatan and the English, by obeying her father's will. This is more clearly explained in Chapter Three.

When the woman of his heart died, Matoaka was all Wahunsenaca had remaining of the woman he had cherished. Due to Wahunsenaca's great love for his beloved wife, he often called his daughter Pocahontas after her mother, for her mother's name was Pocahontas.[3] Pocahontas means "laughing and joyous one."

There was no question that Pocahontas was his favorite child. It is as if he said to himself, "I really have to go all out and love this baby because I lost everything I had to get her!" It was that type of love. If the baby had been a boy, he would have been a special boy, but it was more special because Pocahontas was a female. She resembled her mother, making Wahunsenaca especially caring as a father.

Wahunsenaca decided that it would be better for little Pocahontas to be nurtured by the women in the Mattaponi tribe than at Werowocomoco. The people of the Mattaponi village were her closest relatives and they would give her special attention and tender care because she was a part of them. Little Pocahontas needed breast milk. Her aunts and cousins, who were nursing, were more than willing to nurture little Pocahontas. They had a special love for her. In essence, Wahunsenaca felt like they would nurture little Pocahontas as their own child.

It was the way of the Powhatan people to care for those in need, such as the elderly, widows, and orphans. To take in a relative in need went unquestioned, so the baby was welcomed with enthusiasm and love. Instead of one mother, Pocahontas had many, as the women of the tribe took turns nursing her. This may be one reason why as a child she became so friendly with everyone.

Little Pocahontas was not the only child born to Wahunsenaca and his wife Pocahontas. Little Pocahontas had numerous older brothers and sisters by her parents. Little Pocahontas was born late in her parents' lives. Most of her older full brothers and sisters were adults and held prominent positions in Powhatan society. Her eldest full sister, Mattachanna, was married to Uttamattamakin, a priest of the highest order.[4]

Their names reveal their tribal affiliations and social status. Mattachanna came from the Mattaponi tribe; *Matta*, as in the name of the Mattaponi tribe, is attached to *channa*, the root of her personal name. Uttamattamakin's name signifies that he was from the Uttamusak Temple, the highest temple for the Powhatan nation, which housed the highest order of Powhatan *quiakros* (priests), and was also from the Mattaponi tribe. The *Utta* in Uttamattamakin's name signifies his association with the Uttamusak Temple. *Utta* is followed by *matta*, which also indicates his association with the Mattaponi tribe.

Two of little Pocahontas's elder brothers by her Mattaponi mother were chiefs. Parahunt was the chief of the Powhatan tribe; the Powhatan tribe was the headquarters of the priests, or *quiakros* [kē-ä-krōs].[5] Pochins was chief of the Kecoughtan tribe.[6] There could have been more; some of them may have been in the priesthood line. Wahunsenaca set them in higher positions.

Being related to Wahunsenaca brought on expectations of setting a good example to the Powhatan people. Greater responsibilities and duties rested on the shoulders of Wahunsenaca's family members.

After little Pocahontas was weaned, her father, Wahunsenaca, requested she live with him at the capital village of Werowocomoco, where her eldest full sister, Mattachanna, cared for her.

Everyone loved little Pocahontas for her laughing and joyous nature. Although Wahunsenaca had other children by Pocahontas's mother and children by his alliance wives, he had a special love for Pocahontas, and she, in return, had a special love and respect for her father. She was always doing something to make her father laugh—a gesture, perhaps, that would remind him of her mother, not necessarily because the behavior was similar, but he would remember his wife and love Pocahontas all the more because of the fact that she came from the mother who died for Wahunsenaca to have her. Little Pocahontas brightened Wahunsenaca's heart.

He was also very protective of Pocahontas. He saw that Pocahontas was watched over carefully, and he kept her close to him. By the time Pocahontas was ten years old, the bond between father and daughter had grown deep and strong.

So enduring was her love for her father that the story of Pocahontas cannot be told without talking about Wahunsenaca. All their actions were motivated by their love for each other. Wahunsenaca did everything he could to protect his daughter. In all that she did, through all that she endured, Pocahontas was guided by her love and respect for her father and for her people. Her love for her father never wavered, even though events to come would force them both onto a tragic path.

CHAPTER TWO
Captain John Smith: An English Chief

Pocahontas was about ten years old[1] when the English colonists arrived in Tsenacomoca[2] during the spring of 1607. She was living with her father at Werowocomoco, the secular capital of the Powhatan nation. Her father, Chief Powhatan Wahunsenaca, was the paramount chief of the Powhatan nation.

Seventeenth-century Powhatan society had a clear division between childhood and adulthood. The distinction was marked by physical appearance as well as what types of behavior were permitted or not allowed. Physical appearance was evident in clothing—or the lack thereof—and hairstyle. Children could go naked and barefoot until they started coming of age. Their hair was not cut until they came of age. There were also distinct things that a child was not allowed to participate in.

These cultural standards applied to Wahunsenaca's children as well. As a child, Pocahontas could not have surpassed the cultural boundaries pertaining to children. Regardless of how deep Wahunsenaca's affections were for Pocahontas, even he would not have expected the *quiakros* (priests), warriors, or adult women to bend the social rules for Pocahontas. Instead of spoiling the children of chiefs, people expected more responsibility and discipline of them. To meet these high standards, children of chiefs were provided more supervision and training.

Contrary to popular stereotypes, Powhatan children did not run wild. They were watched over with attention and care. Children ensured the continuity of the Powhatan people. They were protected from harm by all possible means. Being a member of the royal family, Pocahontas would have been supervised at all times. She may have been provided even more security due to her favored status with her father.

Captain John Smith was twenty-seven years old when he

arrived with the other colonists in the land they often referred to as the New World. He was not an upper-class Englishman of high social status. Instead, he was an adventurer.

The English colonists called Pocahontas's father Chief Powhatan or simply Powhatan. They did not understand why the paramount chief had different names. Besides Chief Powhatan or Wahunsenaca, he was also called Mamanatowick, Ottaniack, as well as Werowance Powhatan Wahunsenaca. The English colonists did not understand that Wahunsenaca was his personal name, whereas the other terms referred to his political position as paramount chief. For instance, today the term *president* in the context of the president of the United States is a positional name, whereas the personal name of the president changes according to who is in office. *Mamanatowick* and *ottaniack* are nongendered positional terms that the Powhatan people used to refer to the paramount chief. On the other hand, *werowance* is a gender-specific Powhatan word. *Wero* translates as "secular leader" or "commander," whereas the ending *-ance* indicates that the commander is a male. A female leader would be called a *werowancesquaw*, ending in *-squaw*. In order to distinguish the paramount chief from a tribal or village chief, often the word *Powhatan* would be used after the word *werowance*. The word *Powhatan* was the name of the nation. Thus, *Werowance Powhatan* means "male commander of the Powhatan nation." Wahunsenaca was his personal name.

The Powhatan nation comprised six original tribes[3] with other tribes in its alliance, together totaling more than thirty tribes. Most of the tribes had their own secular chief, or *werowance*. An alliance tribe did not have to have a *werowance*, but every village that came under the Powhatan structure had to have at least one, if not more, *quiakro*, or Powhatan priest. If a village did not already have a *quiakro*, priests would be set up in that village for them from the larger pool of *quiakros* within the Powhatan nation. However, most of these incoming villages already had priests who were familiar with the ways of the Powhatan priests because they communicated with each other. They all spoke the Algonquian language, and the dialect was the same as with any other tribe of the Powhatan nation.

The political structure in the Powhatan nation was balanced between the *werowances*, secular chiefs, and the *quiakros*, the Powhatan priests. The *quiakros* held the power to accept or reject proposals made during council among the secular chiefs. In essence, the *quiakros* had the final word.[4]

The *quiakros* held different positions within the Powhatan society. Some were spiritual leaders, political advisors, medical doctors, historians, and they enforced Powhatan norms of behavior. Another job of the *quiakros* was to gain, maintain, and analyze intelligence information. They would circulate through the villages to catch the tone of the villagers, hear what was being said, and monitor situations. They paid close attention to the movement of outside tribes and the actions of Europeans.

When the English colonists reached the shores of Powhatan land, various Powhatan *werowances*, tribal chiefs, sought to entertain them and procure friendly relations and trade.[5] Meanwhile, the *quiakros* kept a close watch on the English colonists and began discussing the situation of their arrival and their building a fort. The *quiakros* had to decide how to contain the English colonists. Rather than going in and destroying the English colonists, which they could have done in the first days of the colonists' arrival, the *quiakros* wanted to try to contain them, to make them allies and part of the Powhatan nation. Wahunsenaca and the *quiakros* were in agreement in this strategy. Thus, from the Powhatan perspective, the Powhatan showed friendship to the English colonists from the beginning of their arrival.

Approximately six months later, during the winter of 1607, English colonist Smith took some men with him to explore the territory. They ventured deeper inside the territory of Tsenacomoca along the Chickahominy River. Powhatan warriors were out hunting for food when they discovered the colonists. By this time, the presence of the English fort on Jamestown Island was well known among the Powhatan people. A skirmish ensued, ending with Smith being taken captive by Opechancanough[6] and the party of Powhatan warriors.[7]

Opechancanough was a younger brother of Wahunsenaca, and he was the *werowance* of the Pamunkey. Most of the Powhatan warriors were probably Pamunkey because the Pamunkey at that time had more warriors than any other tribe. It is likely that there were also warriors from the Youghtanund and the Mattaponi tribes because they lived in close proximity to each other and often worked together.

Many of the Powhatan people were afraid of the English because they used "thunder sticks" to kill them. They had begun to believe that Smith was like a deity because of his gun and sword. When Smith went into any village, he would take four or five armed English colonists with him. They would traumatize the people with their weapons to the point that they would give Smith what he wanted to get him to leave. For instance, Smith would pretend to come into a village in a friendly manner. When he was in close proximity to the chief of the village, he would put his pistol to the chief's head, demanding a ransom of food in exchange for the chief's release. Smith and his men would proceed to take all the corn and food in the village. As they left, Smith would throw down a few blue beads, claiming to have "traded" with the Powhatan people.

Opechancanough took Smith around to various villages to demonstrate to our people that he was as human as the Powhatan were. The purpose was to show that Smith did not possess supernatural powers, to demonstrate that he was not a deity. Opechancanough proved that Smith was a mortal because the Powhatan were able to capture him, indicating that Smith was not out of their domain of control. It is most likely that the directive to Opechancanough to take Smith around to the villages came from Pocahontas's father, Wahunsenaca, after consulting with the *quiakros*. The *quiakros* did not like the fact that our people were deifying Smith.

After taking Smith to various Powhatan villages, Opechancanough escorted him to Werowocomoco to meet with Wahunsenaca. Pocahontas was living in Werowocomoco during this time. Whether Pocahontas knew of Smith's capture is uncertain. During their meeting, Wahunsenaca asked Smith why the English had come to his land. Smith told him that they had been in a battle with the Spanish. They came into his territory to escape the Spanish.[8]

The Powhatan were uneasy about the Spanish. Their presence had been both rumored and experienced since the late fifteenth century. The Spanish had become rich at the cost of death, destruction, and slavery of Native people of South and North America. In South America, Native people had been enslaved to work in the silver and gold mines controlled by the Spanish. Natives in North America fared somewhat better due to the lack of finding gold, which reduced the intensity of Spanish intrusions.

Still, Native people in North America had experienced a degree of the cruelty of Spaniards as well. The actions of Hernando de Soto in the sixteenth century were so horrendous, Native people in North America called the Spaniards the "sons of the devil."[9] In addition, although it was not intentional, the Spanish conquistadors introduced European diseases to North America, wiping out large populations of the Native people in the southeastern region of the present-day United States.

De Soto's march did not reach as far north as Powhatan territory, but he and his men came close, turning westward south of present-day Virginia. The Powhatan certainly felt the effects and heard of the news of the Spaniards.[10]

Later, when the primary focus of the Spanish was south of the Powhatan nation, Spanish ships patrolled the Atlantic coast, at times capturing Native people. In 1559 or 1560, a young Powhatan male in line to be chief—who later came to be called Don Luis—boarded a Spanish ship. The Spanish writings indicate that it was by mutual consent, with an agreement that the young male would be returned shortly.[11] Mattaponi oral history does not say whether he was taken captive or if he went willingly. Still, it is known that the Spanish often took Native people captive against their will, which would have instilled in the Native people more animosity toward the Spanish.

Contrary to misconceptions about the Native people of North America, communication, travel, and networking were widespread. The Powhatan knew more of what was happening in the world than they are often given credit for. After Luis returned to his homeland—nearly eleven years later—they learned a great deal about international events as well. He had been taught Spanish by the Spanish Jesuit priests. In addition to being taken to Spain, he was also taken to Spanish colonies in present-day Mexico.

Eventually, Luis was able to convince the Spanish to return him to his homeland in the early 1570s. But he was not allowed to return home alone. Instead, a small group of Spanish Jesuit priests insisted upon staying in Luis's homeland. Some Jesuit priests were terrified that Luis would revert to his "pagan" ways. Luis had been returned to his homeland because he had said that he would teach his people the Spanish religion.

Upon their arrival, Luis was immediately recognized. His brother had stepped in for him as chief while he was away, but Luis was told that he was the legitimate paramount chief. Upon hearing this news from his people, he responded by saying that it would not be necessary for his brother to step down for him because he had come to teach them spiritual matter.

It was not long, however, before Luis retreated from the

Spanish Jesuits' camp. He went back to live among his family. In the meantime, the Spanish Jesuit priests became ill with the same disease that had wiped out enormous portions of the Native population in North America. The Powhatan leaders and the *quiakros* decided that the Jesuit priests must be killed in order to prevent another crisis epidemic. Luis participated in this action to protect the Powhatan people.

As a result, relations between the Spanish and the Powhatan grew hostile. When the Spanish discovered that their Jesuit priests had been killed, they demanded that Luis be turned over to them. With Luis being of the royal paramount chief line, the Powhatan refused; consequently, the Spanish soldiers indiscriminately captured about ten Powhatan men, placed them on trial, and hung them from their ship. Afterward, the Spanish promised to return with further retaliations.[12]

The Spanish threat influenced Wahunsenaca to both build alliances with the regional tribes, enlarging the Powhatan nation, and to make friends with the English when they arrived in 1607. According to Mattaponi sacred oral history, Luis and Wahunsenaca were the same person. The Spanish wanted the Powhatan to hand Luis over to them to put him to death. They had vowed to return. Consequently, when the English arrived with weaponry equivalent to the Spanish, which the Powhatan did not have, Wahunsenaca desired to have them as an allied tribe within the Powhatan nation. He was concerned that the Spanish would come again, as they had before, with diseases and killing people with their guns.

The English and the Spanish were rival enemies. The English had been robbing Spanish ships, literally sponsoring pirate attacks against the Spanish. The Spanish certainly did not want the English to establish colonies in the "New World." As a result, the English colonists were very leery of the Spanish.

The English colonists chose Jamestown Island more for

its strategic position against the Spanish than as a defense against the Powhatan.[13] It was farther upriver, around a bend, out of site from the bay. With the Spanish being the dominant European colonizers in the New World, who often patrolled the Atlantic coastline, the English did not want their first fort to be in plain sight of any Spanish ships entering Chesapeake Bay.

Although Jamestown was strategically located to protect the English from the Spanish, it was a poor place to inhabit, which explains why there were no Powhatan villages on the island. The Powhatan people used the area for hunting. Jamestown Island was not suitable for sustaining village life. Mosquitoes were numerous and the water was brackish.[14] It also lacked abundant food that was easily found east and west of Jamestown along the river. Many of the hardships the English colonists later endured stemmed from this poor choice of a site on which to build a fort.

According to Mattaponi sacred oral history, Wahunsenaca truly liked Smith. He offered Smith a position to be a *werowance* of the English colonists, to be the leader of the English within the Powhatan nation.[15] In addition, Wahunsenaca told Smith that the English could live and settle in a more habitable place in the Powhatan nation than on Jamestown Island. Wahunsenaca offered Capahowasick[16] as a place in which the English colonists could live. This area had freshwater, plenteous seafood, and was adequately navigable for their ships. Wahunsenaca was letting the whole English settlement come in to be a part of Powhatan society. He was giving them a place to stay east of Werowocomoco on the eastern shore,* possibly at the mouth of the Pamunkey (York) River. Wahunsenaca thought that with the English ships and ammunition in that area, the Spanish would not come into their territory. Establishing an English settlement east of

* Virginia's eastern shore is considered to be the land peninsula extending between the Chesapeake Bay and the Atlantic Ocean.

Werowocomoco would provide a protective barrier from the Spanish for the Powhatan secular capital. Also, the English colonists could act as an intermediary between England and the Powhatan for trading. He viewed the English at that time as having come in peace. They were welcome to stay as long as they wished. "Stay here, make your home here" is what Wahunsenaca was saying to the English colonists. That was the significance of Smith being made a *werowance*.

The English ships were big in comparison to the Powhatan canoes. They could handle the ocean and Chesapeake Bay. The canoes, banded together, in which Wahunsenaca would travel over to the eastern shore, were slow and the travel entailed some danger. When storms came up and the waters got rough, waves could reach six to eight feet high. So he felt that the English ships would do better than the canoes there.

If the Spanish came in, they would then have to face the English-Powhatan people from the east, as well as the Powhatan from the west. The Spanish would be caught in between. Wahunsenaca was considering that when he made these offers to Smith, because the English had weaponry equal to the Spanish.

Although Smith alleged years later that Pocahontas saved his life during a four-day ceremony in the process of his being made a Powhatan *werowance*, his life was never in danger. His life did not need saving. Why would the Powhatan want to kill a person they were initiating to be a *werowance*? By Smith's own admission, Wahunsenaca gave Smith his word that Smith would be released in four days.[17] Smith's fears was either a figment of his own imagination or an embellishment to dramatize his narrative.

The *quiakros* played an integral part in such a ceremony. Children, male or female, were not allowed to attend. Children were not allowed into a religious ritual entailing priests. The *quiakros* were highly respected persons. They were regarded as being next to Ahone, the Good and Great Spirit. This must be understood in order to put these aspects into perspective. Pocahontas would not have been in the ceremony to throw herself on top of Smith to save him because the *quiakros* would not have allowed Pocahontas to be there. It is important to keep in mind that there were a large number of *quiakros* at the Werowocomoco village because it was the secular capital of the Powhatan nation. Some of the highest and oldest *quiakros*, the most respected of the *quiakros*, would have been there, especially Uttamattamakin. The ceremony with Smith was not secular, because the *quiakros* were participating.

After being initiated as a *werowance* over the English colony, not only was Smith now considered a member of Powhatan society, but the entire English colony were considered members. It demonstrates how much the English were welcomed by the Powhatan. In the course of their discussions, Smith promised Wahunsenaca to protect the Powhatan people from the Spanish.[18]

Pocahontas keenly felt love and loyalty both to her father, Wahunsenaca, and to her people. With Smith's position as a *werowance*, Pocahontas would have expected Smith to be loyal to her father and people. As a *werowance*, Pocahontas considered Smith a leader, a defender of the Powhatan. Pocahontas saw Smith the same way her father saw him—as an allied chief of the English tribe, under and part of the Powhatan nation. As part of the Powhatan nation, the English tribe could readily expand Powhatan trade to England, which the *quiakros* and Wahunsenaca much desired.

Smith and Pocahontas's father, Wahunsenaca, pledged their friendship to each other. In Powhatan society, one's word is one's bond. A bond is considered sacred. Our people could not conceive of deception because one keeps one's word. Our people, including Pocahontas, did not perceive deception within Smith; however, it later became clear that he had no intention of honoring this new relationship. Yet, true to his word, Wahunsenaca released Smith after the four days transpired.

Upon Smith's return to the English fort, it was the English colonists who truly sought to kill him. After a quick trial, Smith was sentenced to death. Captain Christopher Newport arrived from England that evening and put a stop to the execution. In reality, Smith was saved from the English colonists by Newport, not by Wahunsenaca or Pocahontas.[19]

CHAPTER THREE

Pocahontas: The Powhatan Peace Symbol

Chief Powhatan Wahunsenaca and the Powhatan people welcomed the English colonists when they arrived in 1607. They
entertained them with food and hospitality. They allowed the
English to build their fort on Powhatan hunting grounds that the
English called Jamestown. Wahunsenaca wanted to make friends
with them. He welcomed the English with open arms. When the
English fell on hard times during the first winter, he sent envoys
with food to Jamestown.

The English colonists were ill prepared for life in the New
World. Their way of living in Europe did not prepare them for the
way of living according to the ecosystem in the Powhatan territory. The English did not pack enough food when they came over,
and although the land was bountiful, the English were lazy. They
wanted the food to be given to them, to have someone else do the
work for them.

Wahunsenaca, seeing that the English were not prepared
or equipped to endure their new environment, allowed his tribes
to take food to the English settlers. He often sent envoys to the
Jamestown fort with food. The Powhatan way, especially among
leaders, was to constantly seek the good of the whole tribe. This is
one of the main aspects that constituted a good person. Greed and
selfish ambition were considered bad. To aspire to seek one's own
personal welfare over the concern of the tribe was frowned upon;
consequently, the sharing of food and showing hospitality was the
norm among the Powhatan people. Thus, the generous hospitality
to the English in the early stages of their arrival came naturally to
the Powhatan.

Wahunsenaca's agreement with Captain John Smith
sealed the friendship and bond between the Powhatan people
and the English, providing all the more reasons for the Powha-

tan to send food to the starving colonists during their first winter. In confidence and trust in Smith as the *werowance* (chief) of the English colonists, Wahunsenaca allowed his favorite daughter, Pocahontas, to accompany these entourages. Pocahontas was closely chaperoned and watched over by the *quiakros* (priests) and warriors. But if Wahunsenaca had feared for her safety, she would not have been allowed to go.

As a result, the English colonists became familiar with Pocahontas, the paramount chief's favorite daughter. They associated her with the gifts of food. But the food was actually coming from the leader of the Powhatan people, Wahunsenaca. As a child, Pocahontas's abilities to accomplish what the English colonists attributed to her were very unlikely.

Many popular stories about Pocahontas portray her taking food to the English colonists at Jamestown of her own accord; however, Pocahontas was a child. She was about ten years old when the English colonists arrived in the spring of 1607. We know that Pocahontas had not yet come of age because she dressed and acted as a child. She was still playing childhood games at that time. For instance, seventeenth-century writings state that Pocahontas played and did cartwheels with the young English boys within the walls of the English fort. This reveals that Pocahontas had not yet reached puberty. When young people of the Powhatan nation reached puberty, they stopped cartwheeling. The English writings also say that she was naked.[1] Powhatan children often wore little clothing in the summer. In the summer months, Pocahontas was a virtually naked little girl until she came of age. (In the winter, Pocahontas would have worn a covering to protect her from the cold.) As a child, Pocahontas would not have been allowed to travel by herself or leave her village without her father's permission. The *quiakros* would not have allowed Pocahontas the privilege of going over to Jamestown anytime she wanted to either.

Numerous popular stories about Pocahontas also imply that she lived close enough to Jamestown to walk there anytime she desired. She did not live close to Jamestown at all. She lived at Werowocomoco with her father. Reaching Jamestown from Werowocomoco required crossing the wide Pamunkey (York) River and traveling approximately twelve miles by foot. The other way to reach Jamestown from Werowocomoco would have been by canoe all the way. This would have been even more dangerous than crossing the river and making the trek by land. It is absurd to think that Pocahontas could have made the dangerous journey alone.

Pocahontas did go to Jamestown, but she went under the permission and protection provided by her father, Wahunsenaca. Being a member of the Powhatan paramount chief family, Pocahontas was always chaperoned by warriors and/or *quiakros*. The *quiakros* sometimes accompanied her undercover, not disclosing their positions as priests to the English colonists. Bodyguards constantly watched over little Pocahontas. The English colonists may or may not have recognized them. She was constantly watched over, even at Werowocomoco. Being the paramount chief's favorite daughter, the bodyguards would have been watching her even more closely when they traveled to Jamestown. It is possible the English colonists realized Wahunsenaca's affection for her because of the tight security that always accompanied Pocahontas to the fort.

The conceptions of Pocahontas bringing food or having led other Powhatan people to bring food to the English colonists of her own accord and against her father's wishes are false. Being the daughter of Wahunsenaca, Pocahontas may have had certain privileges and liberties that other females did not have; however, her freedoms were still limited. As a child, she could not have moved outside the realm of restrictions placed on children in Powhatan society. Children in Powhatan society, even of the royal Powhatan family, did not have command over male or female adults. It was not permitted in Powhatan culture. Pocahontas could not have ordered male warriors to escort her to Jamestown.

Traveling to Jamestown would have required the assistance of Powhatan men. The Pamunkey River is very wide around the location of Werowocomoco. The Powhatan traveled the waterways in large dugout canoes. These canoes, made out of large trees, could easily weigh 400 pounds. Pocahontas, a ten-year-old girl, would not have been able to handle such a canoe all by herself for such a long distance. The danger of high waves in storms significantly reduced the probabilities of Powhatan women traveling beyond the shoreline in a dugout canoe.

Instead, the Powhatan entourage brought *her* as a peace gesture from her father. Pocahontas did not take food to the English colonists against her father's wishes; she was *allowed* to go, under supervision, with the Powhatan ambassadors, because of the privilege of being the highest *werowance*'s daughter and to demonstrate that the Powhatan came in peace. The fact that Pocahontas was part of the Powhatan entourage reveals that Wahunsenaca had no intention of attacking the English fort; otherwise, Pocahontas would not have been with them.

The Powhatan entourage visited the English to discuss matters of stately business.[2] Pocahontas did not *lead* the company going to Jamestown. Instead, Pocahontas was often put in front of the Powhatan envoy as they approached the English fort to demonstrate that they came in peace.

At that time, it was customary to bring a child along and to place that child in the lead to show that the visit was meant for official business. If there were only warriors and possibly some *quiakros*, another tribe might misinterpret the intentions of the approaching group. But if a child accompanied the entourage, particularly a female child, it was known that the approach was in peace. This tactic was especially helpful when there was a language barrier.

Pocahontas was the ideal and foremost female child to go to Jamestown. Not having a mother was part of the reason that Pocahontas was outgoing and more mature in conduct, but at the same time, she was not left without love, because her father made up for it and made her feel important. Pocahontas was a very outgoing, bright, and confident young lady. She could do anything a young male could do. Her father and the *quiakros* recognized that.

Pocahontas did not go to the English with the purpose of formally teaching Smith, as some popular myths propagate. It is possible that Pocahontas engaged in a dialogue with Smith while she was at Jamestown. Smith could have asked her, "What does this word mean?" It could have been any Powhatan word that Smith did not know. Being friendly, Pocahontas would try to answer his questions. As a famous saying, my father, Chief Daniel Webster "Little Eagle" Custalow, used to say to me, "Son, a stranger is simply a friend you have not yet met." Pocahontas had no fear of the English—the English were simply friends she had not yet met. Because she was a very bright girl, she would try to provide the Powhatan word for the object in question. She was quick to learn English as well. It is possible that the English relied on Pocahontas for help with communication and interpretation.

Pocahontas was also not a spy for the Powhatan, as some scholars have asserted.[3] Just as the English colonists may have been trying to obtain Powhatan knowledge from Pocahontas, Smith recognized that Pocahontas's father was relying on her for information about the colonists. Her father may have talked to her about her experiences at the English fort, but this is not to say that Pocahontas was a spy for her father. There is no foundation for Pocahontas being a spy. She was not a spy; she was a child. She came to show peace, to show that the adults came in peace.

The Powhatan who gathered information about the English colonists would have been the *quiakros* who went to Jamestown as well. They came to survey the English village, not as spies to take over or to devise ways to kill off the English. The *quiakros* were looking to see if there were any aspects of the English culture they could use to improve the Powhatan way of life. The *quiakros* were also ascertaining whether it was possible for the English to become part of the Powhatan nation, which is what the *quiakros* wanted. This is why Wahunsenaca made so many kind gestures and generous offers to Smith, whom they thought was the leader of the English tribe.

As Wahunsenaca's favorite child, Pocahontas being allowed to go with the delegations to Jamestown demonstrated his sincerity to befriend the English colonists. As a child, and a female at that, her presence conveyed the message that the Powhatan party came in peace. In this way, Pocahontas held a special position among her people. By letting his own daughter lead the entourage, Pocahontas became a peace symbol of her father and of the Powhatan people. Pocahontas was the Powhatan symbol of peace.

CHAPTER FOUR
Powhatan Rule: Not by Force

During the summer of 1608, the relationship between the Powhatan and the English colonists began to deteriorate due to the ongoing contentious behavior of the English colonists toward the Powhatan tribes. Captain John Smith, the new Powhatan *werowance* (chief) of the English tribe, began rudely demanding corn from the Powhatan villages in Tsenacomoca. Strain intensified due to summer droughts, decreasing the production of the Powhatan harvests. The English colonists did not make adequate efforts to plant their own crops. Smith and his men became violent and excessively greedy. After being warmly welcomed into a village, Smith would pull his pistol on the chief and would often take all the corn in the village. A Mattaponi woman chided Smith's greed, saying, "You call yourself a Christian, yet you leave us with no food for the winter!"[1]

In January 1609, Smith made a detour during his rounds of securing food for the Jamestown fort by going to Werowocomoco. He arrived in the Powhatan capital village without giving prior notice. Powhatan carriers were sent out to notify Chief Powhatan Wahunsenaca. Wahunsenaca put aside what he was doing and returned to Werowocomoco. (Mattaponi oral history does not say precisely where he was at that time. Just as with the president today, there are numerous places where he could have been. He could have been away for business, such as meeting with other chiefs in another village. He could have been away hunting. Or he could have been away for spiritual renewal, such as going to the Uttamussac Temple.)

During their visit, Wahunsenaca scolded Smith for his bad behavior. "I have not treated any of my *werowances* as well as you, yet you are the worst *werowance* I have!"[2] Wahunsenaca also expressed his desire for peace. He explained to Smith the

Powhatan philosophy of acquiring more through respectful and peaceful means than through war and the demonstration of force, stating:

> Why do you take by force [that which] you may quickly have by love? Or to destroy them that provide you food? What can you get by war when we can hide our provision and fly to the woods? ... Think you that I am so simple not to know it is better to eat good meat, lie well, and sleep quietly with my women and children, laugh and be merry with you, have copper, hatchets, or what I want, being your friend, than be forced to fly from all?[3]

Yet, according to Smith, Wahunsenaca wanted to kill him during this visit. Once again, Smith alleged that Pocahontas saved his life.[4] Smith claimed that she came to him in the night to warn him of her father's plot to kill him. Due to the tidal currents and the ice on the Pamunkey (York) River, Smith and his men were unable to leave until morning. After Smith and his men stayed all night in Werowocomoco, Smith provided no evidence to substantiate his propagated suspicions and fears.[5] Smith's men were not poisoned. The Powhatan warriors whom he forced to taste the food first did not die. No one attacked them during the night. No one tried to prevent Smith and his men from leaving in the morning. Instead, the Powhatan carried loads of corn to their ship for them. As before, when Smith was made a *werowance* by Wahunsenaca a year prior to this encounter, Smith's own writings do not correspond to his own fears and claims of being saved by Pocahontas.

Once again, according to Mattaponi sacred oral history, Smith's claim of Pocahontas having saved—or, in this case, warned—him do not seem possible within the cultural standards of seventeenth-century Powhatan society. Pocahontas warning Smith in the night implies that Pocahontas, a young girl, was capable of slipping out in the cold night past all adult supervision. According to Mattaponi sacred oral history, this is unlikely. Powhatan children were watched closely and learned discipline early in life. They were not allowed to explore and wander about on their own, especially on an icy cold night. There was always the possibility of being attacked by wild animals. It was treacherous and dangerous for a warrior, much less for a female child. Pocahontas, being the favorite daughter of Wahunsenaca, was watched even more closely than other children. She was constantly guarded and protected. More important, if Wahunsenaca truly wanted to kill Smith and his men at Werowocomoco during the nighttime, it would have been very unlikely that Pocahontas could have been able to get past the Powhatan warriors who were guarding them.

To confuse matters further, Smith wrote that Wahunsenaca had put out a death warrant on him. If this was so, why did Smith then travel deeper into Powhatan territory to the Pamunkey villages the next morning instead of returning to Jamestown?[6] Either Smith was so confident in his ability to defend himself from the Powhatan or there was no reasonable threat to his life, which is the position of Mattaponi scared oral history. The Powhatan were not trying to kill Smith.

Smith's writings continued to assert that the Powhatan were trying to kill him. Smith claimed that Opechancanough had planned to ambush him and his men at a Pamunkey village upriver from Werowocomoco.[7] Smith reported that he was able to outmaneuver Opechancanough and the large number of Powhatan warriors; consequently, Smith implied that he and his men were brave, courageous, and strategically shrewd.

Meanwhile, Wahunsenaca sent the European traders— called Dutchmen in the English writings—living in or near

Werowocomoco to Jamestown. These Dutchmen were in the Werowocomoco area in order to build Wahunsenaca an English-style house. As traders, they were more sympathetic toward the Powhatan than the English colonists. At Jamestown, the Dutchmen acquired goods such as swords and gunshot, which the Powhatan tribes desired.[8] These were the types of goods that Smith would neither provide nor trade with the Powhatan. Smith's refusal to trade went against the behavior Wahunsenaca expected of his *werowances*. By using the Dutchmen, Wahunsenaca found a way to get what he wanted by other means—notably without the use of force or violence.

If these two events were indeed life threatening, as Smith's account claimed, if they were even remotely accurate in intention and motivation, Smith was certainly brave and savvy. However, if his fear of being killed was not in sync with the true Powhatan intentions, Smith either twisted the events to make them appear as though he was courageous or as though the Powhatan warriors were not strong opponents.

There are two sets of writings by Smith regarding Jamestown. The first publication was a letter he wrote in 1608. The letter was sent by ship to a friend in England. Without Smith's knowledge, the letter was published, titled "A True Relation." The second set consists of extensive writing on Jamestown history and was published in 1624. At this time, many of the people who could have disputed Smith, such as Pocahontas and Wahunsenaca, were no longer alive. The earlier writing by Smith in 1608 does not mention either Pocahontas saving his life during a ceremony (his initiation into the Powhatan society as a *werowance*) or her sneaking around in the darkness of night to warn him. It is not until Smith's "Generall Historie of Virginia," published in 1624, that Pocahontas was credited with saving his life.

Why would Smith produce two accounts consisting of contrasting implications? It is possible that Smith's 1624 publication was motivated by the political climate of the day. It is significant that the writings were published shortly after the "Uprising of 1622," the first unquestionably serious attack on the English colonists by the Powhatan.* It had a devastating effect on the English colonists. Nearly a fourth of the English-colonists' population perished in one day. Smith may have been attempting to console the English colonists that the Powhatan could be defeated. Perhaps it was self-promotion. Either way, by Smith's 1624 account, he had taken on both Wahunsenaca and Opechancanough in their own territories and emerged victorious. Most of the prominent Powhatan people who could dispute Smith's claims were no longer alive. Besides, after the Powhatan attack in 1622, it is unlikely the English would have been inclined to listen to the Powhatan perspective.

---

* The "Uprising of 1622"—from the English-colonist perspective, it has often been referred to as the "Massacre of 1622"—was the first full outright war by the Powhatan waged upon the English colonists. It took place on Good Friday, the Friday before Easter Sunday in the Christian tradition. The Powhatan people, then under the leadership of Chief Opechancanough, made a surprise and devastating attack on the English colonists, killing nearly one-fourth of the English population. However, the attack was not sustained—it lasted for one day only.[9]

CHAPTER FIVE

Danger in Pocahontas's Homeland

The ways of the Powhatan and the English colonists were very different. The English did not understand the ways of our people. In Powhatan society, children went unclothed, and women were frequently bare-breasted; therefore, seeing a woman's breasts did not excite a warrior. It was a normal way of dress that was built into societal customs. The European men who came over, on the other hand, were all flustered with that which was natural from the Powhatan perspective.

The Powhatan nation was a priestly driven society. As such, the *quiakros* (priests) did not permit sexual misconduct. Rape was not tolerated in Powhatan society. If a male was determined guilty of rape, he would have been driven away from the Powhatan villages. Although the custom of alliance wives in seventeenth-century Powhatan society appears to be sexual misconduct by most current cultural standards, the custom was not for sexual frivolity. When a tribe chose a maiden for the paramount chief, they had a purpose for the relationship: it was to build political alliances through kinship and to enlarge the population of the Powhatan nation.

The European colonists had different concepts. The sexual safety and security of the Powhatan people drastically declined with the arrival of the English colonists. The women and the children needed protection from being raped by the English settlers. The English would either go after the ones who had more authority over each village or they would take the younger ones. They wanted the prize, either way. Against the English's guns, the Powhatan people had no defense. The adult women would offer themselves to the English to prevent them from sexually assaulting their children. Trying to save their children, the Powhatan women would say, "Take me, take me!" to the English raiders. Meanwhile, the elderly men would attempt to hide the children in the woods, back in the ravines, where the children were told to keep quiet. Children were trained to be obedient to adults; the *quiakros* saw to that. That was the only thing the Powhatan people could do when they realized the English were coming with lust to their villages—to hide the children. There was also the risk that the English would steal our children and sell them as slaves.

The Powhatan and English had different agendas. The English did not understand the very civil and political structure of the Powhatan nation. They did not want to understand it. They wanted to look at the Powhatan people as savages. Because the English considered the Powhatan people savages, they considered it to be okay to kill them and take their land. There has to be some type of conviction. People do not just kill other people without some kind of justification for their conscience, unless they are simply killers, murderers. The term *savage* and its associated ideology is what the English colonists used to justify—to rationalize—their actions.

Our culture was the more civilized of the two in that we sought more peaceful means of living with other human beings and the environment. We were not technologically advanced in terms of guns, swords, and big ships, as the Europeans were. They developed the cannon, then the gun. It is important to understand where the English were coming from and what their intentions were. The English were looking for ways to take, enslave, and kill.

Consider, on the other hand, the Powhatan people whose homes were already here. Their ancestors had moved out of Eurasia to get away from violence, to live more peacefully. We were not looking for evil things, as the English were. We were not as advanced technologically, but we were looking for ways of preserving ecology, of preserving resources, because they were gifts from the Good and Great Spirit, Ahone, who gave them to us to use, but to be used wisely. That is why we call Earth, Mother, because Earth acts like a mother to feed us. So our people act to protect it. We are the people of the ecosystem.

We strove to live by the way of peace, whereas the English were living by force and violence. Chief Powhatan Wahunsenaca told Captain John Smith in a subtle way, with tact, "This is not the way we operate in the Powhatan nation. The Quiyoughcosugh [one order of *quiakros*] do not allow it. We operate in love." That was the difference.

As more English colonists continued to come to Tsenacomoca, their atrocities were growing along with their numbers. Desiring the already cleared land of the Powhatan people, which was usually along the riverbanks, the English wiped out many Powhatan villages along the Powhatan (James) River.

The English colonists either killed or enslaved the Powhatan people in the process of taking control of the cleared Powhatan land. Many of the Powhatan who escaped the attacks on their villages died of starvation because they lacked adequate food supplies.

Powhatan children especially were taken by the English colonists to be their slaves. The English colonists would train the Powhatan children to be their servants, claiming that they would civilize these poor children and teach them the Christian doctrine to save their souls.[1]

Powhatan women were sexually assaulted and raped. The English men even sought to rape the Powhatan children.

The Powhatan people were shocked at the behavior of the English colonists. The Powhatan tribes would set up lookout points to watch for the English coming to raid their villages. The English government offered no legal recourse for acts of violence against the Powhatan people.[2] Due to their own atrocious acts, the English colonists were in constant fear of Wahunsenaca retaliating, for the balance of power still lay with the Powhatan people.

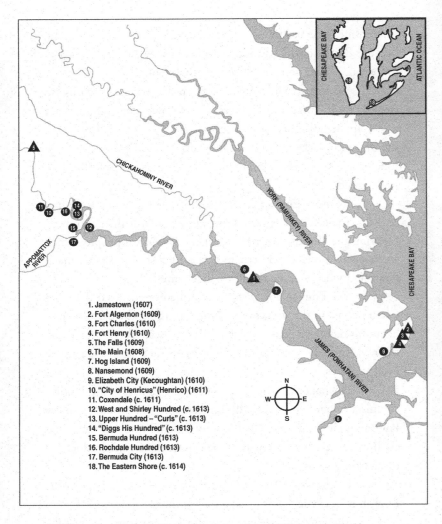

1. Jamestown (1607)
2. Fort Algernon (1609)
3. Fort Charles (1610)
4. Fort Henry (1610)
5. The Falls (1609)
6. The Main (1608)
7. Hog Island (1609)
8. Nansemond (1609)
9. Elizabeth City (Kecoughtan) (1610)
10. "City of Henricus" (Henrico) (1611)
11. Coxendale (c. 1611)
12. West and Shirley Hundred (c. 1613)
13. Upper Hundred – "Curls" (c. 1613)
14. "Diggs His Hundred" (c. 1613)
15. Bermuda Hundred (1613)
16. Rochdale Hundred (1613)
17. Bermuda City (1613)
18. The Eastern Shore (c. 1614)

English settlements in the Powhatan territory from 1607 through 1616.[3]

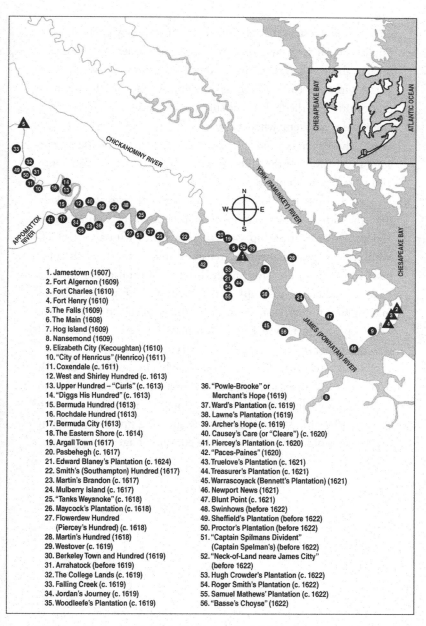

1. Jamestown (1607)
2. Fort Algernon (1609)
3. Fort Charles (1610)
4. Fort Henry (1610)
5. The Falls (1609)
6. The Main (1608)
7. Hog Island (1609)
8. Nansemond (1609)
9. Elizabeth City (Kecoughtan) (1610)
10. "City of Henricus" (Henrico) (1611)
11. Coxendale (c. 1611)
12. West and Shirley Hundred (c. 1613)
13. Upper Hundred – "Curls" (c. 1613)
14. "Diggs His Hundred" (c. 1613)
15. Bermuda Hundred (1613)
16. Rochdale Hundred (1613)
17. Bermuda City (1613)
18. The Eastern Shore (c. 1614)
19. Argall Town (1617)
20. Pasbehegh (c. 1617)
21. Edward Blaney's Plantation (c. 1624)
22. Smith's (Southampton) Hundred (1617)
23. Martin's Brandon (c. 1617)
24. Mulberry Island (c. 1617)
25. "Tanks Weyanoke" (c. 1618)
26. Maycock's Plantation (c. 1618)
27. Flowerdew Hundred
    (Piercey's Hundred) (c. 1618)
28. Martin's Hundred (1618)
29. Westover (c. 1619)
30. Berkeley Town and Hundred (1619)
31. Arrahatock (before 1619)
32. The College Lands (c. 1619)
33. Falling Creek (c. 1619)
34. Jordan's Journey (c. 1619)
35. Woodleefe's Plantation (c. 1619)

36. "Powle-Brooke" or
    Merchant's Hope (1619)
37. Ward's Plantation (c. 1619)
38. Lawne's Plantation (1619)
39. Archer's Hope (c. 1619)
40. Causey's Care (or "Cleare") (c. 1620)
41. Piercey's Plantation (c. 1620)
42. "Paces-Paines" (1620)
43. Truelove's Plantation (c. 1621)
44. Treasurer's Plantation (c. 1621)
45. Warrascoyack (Bennett's Plantation) (1621)
46. Newport News (1621)
47. Blunt Point (c. 1621)
48. Swinhows (before 1622)
49. Sheffield's Plantation (before 1622)
50. Proctor's Plantation (before 1622)
51. "Captain Spilmans Divident"
    (Captain Spelman's) (before 1622)
52. "Neck-of-Land neare James Citty"
    (before 1622)
53. Hugh Crowder's Plantation (c. 1622)
54. Roger Smith's Plantation (c. 1622)
55. Samuel Mathews' Plantation (c. 1622)
56. "Basse's Choyse" (1622)

English settlements in the Powhatan territory by 1622.[4]

As a result, the relations between the Powhatan and the English began to grow tense. By this time, neither Wahunsenaca nor Pocahontas had seen Smith since his visit to Werowocomoco in the winter of 1609. The English colonists had told Pocahontas that Smith had died.[5] But actually, Smith had been injured in a gunpowder accident while he was with his fellow English colonists.[6] The Powhatan did not have any part in the incident. The wound was not life threatening, but it was bad enough to cause him to return to England.[7]

In hindsight, knowing Mattaponi oral history, it is likely that the other English colonists were jealous of Smith's close and powerful relationship with the Powhatan paramount chief. Wahunsenaca was unaware of tensions among the English colonists and their disdain for Smith. Instead, Wahunsenaca and the *quiakros* had perceived Smith as the leader of the English. As such, making him the *werowance* (chief) of the English should not have been a problem; however, the offer may have escalated political tensions between Smith and his countrymen.

As relations between the Powhatan and the English declined, Wahunsenaca stopped allowing Pocahontas to go to the Jamestown fort. He no longer thought she was safe among the English colonists. Pocahontas was growing up, she was about twelve years old. Soon she would be coming of age.

CHAPTER SIX

Pocahontas Comes of Age

During Pocahontas's time, the Powhatan people held rituals for young males and females who were coming of age. The ritual for young males required more time and was more strenuous, but the two had the same purpose: to change one's social status from being a child to being an adult. The male ritual was called a *huskanaw*; the female ritual was called *huskanasquaw*.*[1] Adult males and females played different roles in Powhatan society. After the *huskanaw*, the male's role changes from that of a child to that of man, when he can be accepted into a tribe as a warrior. His allegiances change from his family to his tribe. The female's role changes from that of a child to that of a woman, signifying her eligibility for courtship and marriage.

During their coming-of-age ceremonies, both males and females chose a new name by which to be called to further indicate the identity change. Matoaka, already often called Pocahontas, chose the name of her mother, Pocahontas, during her *huskanasquaw*.

Huskanaws and *huskanasquaws* usually occurred in young people's lives when they were between the ages of twelve and fourteen. Coming-of-age ceremonies normally occurred once a year, at a time that was designated by the *quiakros* (priests) for males and the *quiakros'* wives for females. The sign for a female coming-of-age ceremony would be after she had begun exhibiting signs of female maturity, such as having had several regular menstrual periods. The customary *huskanasquaw* procedures for Pocahontas, since her mother had died at childbirth, were overseen by Pocahontas's full older sister, Mattachanna, who acted as a mother to her.

Because Pocahontas was the favorite daughter of the

---

* The English colonists first mistook the *huskanaw* as child sacrifice.

Powhatan paramount chief, Wahunsenaca, her *huskanasquaw* would have been followed by a major festive occasion in Werowocomoco. Dignitaries from all the tribes under the Powhatan nation would have been invited. However, Wahunsenaca heard through the Powhatan *quiakros*—who were ever watchful of events within the Powhatan society—that the English colonists were plotting to kidnap Pocahontas. Wahunsenaca loved Pocahontas. He wanted to protect her. He had always been very protective of Pocahontas. Consequently, Pocahontas's *huskanasquaw* was more discreet than it would have been otherwise. The guest list was limited to the intimate kinship. Security measures were heightened.

For Pocahontas's coming-of-age ceremony, she would have worn an off-the-shoulder, fringed, soft deerskin dress and deerskin moccasins. Around her neck, she might have worn a necklace made of a strand of seashells. As a member of the royal family, Pocahontas might have worn copper jewelry. She might have worn turkey feathers in her hair, but she would not have been tattooed—members of the paramount chief's family did not tattoo their bodies. Tattooing was for the warriors and the lower classes.

There was a hierarchal status in the Powhatan society. The highest, the elite, were the *quiakros*' families, followed by the paramount chief's family, followed by the lesser chiefs' families, then followed by the warriors' families. The lower status of Powhatan people included the mainstream Powhatan citizens. Minor status distinctions varied from tribe to tribe.

When the young males and females completed their coming-of-age ceremonies, there was much fanfare and dancing. The Powhatan people called these celebrations *pau-waus*, or *pow-wows* today. Children were allowed to attend powwows. Powwows were forms of celebration and thanksgiving. At a powwow, the people would dance, eat, enjoy socializing, and would commemorate Ahone, the Good and Great Spirit, for his protection.

During powwow celebrations, there was a special dance called the *courtship dance*. For Pocahontas, this dance was called the *princess dance*. (Today, it is best known as the princess dance in memory of Pocahontas.) In this dance, single male warriors searched for a mate. Most likely, Kocoum, one of Wahunsenaca's best warriors, asked Pocahontas to dance at this time. After a time of courtship, Pocahontas and Kocoum married.[2]

Wahunsenaca was very pleased to have his beloved daughter, Pocahontas, married to such a fine warrior. Kocoum was ranked in the top fifty warriors who protected Werowocomoco, the capital of the Powhatan nation. These were the elite warriors. It comforted Wahunsenaca to know that his beloved daughter would have such a skilled warrior husband to protect her. Plus, Kocoum was related to one of his closest friends. Kocoum was the younger brother of Chief Japazaw of the Patawomeck tribe, who was a very close friend of Wahunsenaca. The newly married coupled lived at Werowocomoco. While living there with her husband, Pocahontas became pregnant.

During this period, the English colonists continued to destroy Powhatan villages. Fear of danger was rising among the Powhatan, especially along the Powhatan (James) River. A sense of danger was rising in the Powhatan capital as well. The *quiakros* were picking up information indicating that the English colonists were planning to kidnap Pocahontas.

PART TWO

Accounts of Pocahontas's life and death are inaccurate according to tribal history.

—Mattaponi Tribal Member

A Theodor de Bry 1590 edition of a John White drawing.
Courtesy of the Colonial Williamsburg Foundation

CHAPTER SEVEN

Pocahontas Kidnapped

Pocahontas had come of age. Her father had given her in marriage to a special warrior of the Potowomac tribe named Kocoum, a younger brother of Chief Japazaw, one of Chief Powhatan Wahunsenaca's closest friends. Due to rumors that English colonists wanted to kidnap Pocahontas, it was felt by Pocahontas's closest loved ones that it would be wise for Pocahontas to "hide" from the English colonists.[1] Pocahontas and Kocoum were advised to leave Werowocomoco. It was decided that Pocahotnas and Kocoum should go live in Kocoum's home village. His Potowomac village was located near the northern perimeters of Tsenacomoca on the Potomac River. This was the same village in which Japazaw lived. At that time, English colonists did not have any spies in that area, probably due to its remoteness. Pocahontas's family members believed she would be safe there. Wahunsenaca agreed to conceal Pocahontas in her husband's tribe. It is important to keep in mind that Japazaw and Wahunsenaca were very good friends; they were very close. While living among Kocoum's family in the Patawomeck tribe, Pocahontas gave birth to Kocoum's daughter.

The English colonists had spies throughout the Powhatan territory who were looking for Pocahontas under the guise of acting as interpreters and traders. One such spy was living in the Patawomeck region, allegedly to learn their language. This was a somewhat common practice in order to produce translators. However, Mattaponi oral history discloses that in this particular situation, the English colonist was acting as a spy seeking out Pocahontas's location.

Captain Samuel Argall, an English colonist who had arrived in the colony in 1612, was looking for Pocahontas. He heard of Pocahontas's whereabouts through English colonists trading for corn with the Potowomacs in the spring of 1613.[2] Upon learning of Pocahontas's hiding place, Argall quickly prepared his ship for the mission of abducting Pocahontas. He gathered a posse of men and ample weapons. He planned to capture Pocahontas at any cost.

One of Argall's main purposes for coming to the New World was to aid in making the colony a success. Some of the English-colonist leaders had been looking for the whereabouts of Pocahontas in order to capture her. They wanted to capture Pocahontas because they believed her abduction would keep Wahunsenaca from leading an attack against the English colonists. They knew how much he loved his daughter and would not want her to be hurt. The English colonists feared Wahunsenaca would attack them because of their severe treatment of the Powhatan people, such as killing them in order to confiscate their prime agricultural land. Lands along the rivers, such as the Powhatan (James), were especially important. This land had already been cultivated by the Powhatan and was exceptionally fertile.

The plot to abduct Pocahontas was an effort on the part of the English colonists to buy more time. They were required to find a way to be financially profitable and self-sustaining by 1616.[3] Since they had not found gold as they had anticipated, other endeavors were explored, such as glassmaking and tobacco production. Without question, the English colonists wanted to bring in more men and weapons to strengthen their position.

When Argall arrived, he demanded that Japazaw bring Pocahontas on board his ship.[4] The Potowomac chief and *quiakros* (priests) called an emergency meeting of the tribal council.[5] At the same time, Japazaw quickly sent messengers to Wahunsenaca informing him of what Argall was doing. After a long meeting, the council agreed that for the safety of the tribe, there was no choice but to submit to Argall's demands. But at the same time, they would also try to bargain with Argall to release Pocahontas and return her to her husband after she had seen the inside of Argall's ship. Plus, the council maintained that Argall's men had to remain, unarmed, with the council until Pocahontas was returned to them.

Japazaw did not want to hand Pocahontas over to Argall. She was his younger brother's wife. She was a relative and he loved her. He knew that Pocahontas's presence in his territory was an effort by her father to maintain her safety. Japazaw wanted to keep Pocahontas safe. It was his duty. He knew that submitting to Argall's demands would betray his loyalty to the Powhatan.

At the same time, Japazaw knew that Argall would be relentless. He would not give up on his quest to capture Pocahontas. The English had "thunder sticks" and had brutally killed or enslaved many Powhatan people. Japazaw feared for the lives of his people. It was also Japazaw's duty to seek the good of the tribe. If he did not comply with the English captain, Argall would probably have had many of the Potowomac killed.

Japazaw was put in the difficult position of making a decision between the lesser of two evils. The Potowomac had not known the English were coming to abduct Pocahontas. They were neither organized nor prepared to defend themselves against the English, who had come quickly and caught the Potowomac off guard. Even though Japazaw had warriors who could protect him from hand-to-hand combat, he did not have warriors who could protect him from guns and swords.

It is important to try to look at the situation from their standpoint. For the safety of his people, Japazaw did not want to antagonize Argall any further, so he tried to be as friendly as possible and proposed a compromise: Japazaw would let Pocahontas board Argall's ship, but Argall had to promise to release her shortly afterward. Argall agreed, promising to return Pocahontas to the care of the Potowomac as Japazaw had requested. He also reassured Japazaw that he would not harm Pocahontas.

In an attempt to gain Argall's sympathy, Japazaw also told Argall that he feared retaliation from Wahunsenaca.[6] Argall stated that the English would protect the Potowomac tribe if Wahunsenaca attacked them.[7] After these agreements, Japazaw submitted to Argall's demand for Pocahontas. Argall remained with Japazaw while Japazaw's wife went to get Pocahontas.

Once Pocahontas returned with Japazaw's wife, Argall and his men escorted Pocahontas on board the English ship—whereupon Argall quickly broke his word and refused to release Pocahontas. He kept her captive.

Once aboard Argall's ship, Argall ordered that Powhatan messengers be sent to Wahunsenaca with his ransom demands. The ransom demand for Pocahontas's release required the return of the English weapons that had been taken from Jamestown, return of the English prisoners Wahunsenaca held captive, as well a shipment of corn.[8] Japazaw's messenger had arrived earlier; consequently, Pocahontas's father was already aware of the situation before Argall's messenger arrived.

The *quiakros* advised Wahunsenaca to retaliate swiftly and attempt to rescue Pocahontas; however, Wahunsenaca feared Pocahontas would be killed as a result of such a response. He hoped that the English colonists would not harm her. After all, she had visited Jamestown often and was known by them. She had accompanied the Powhatan envoys bringing food and supplies to the colonists. Deep in Wahunsenaca's heart, he could not conceive of the English hurting Pocahontas. He chose instead the path most likely to ensure Pocahontas's safety. Wahunsenaca immediately offered to pay the ransom demanded by Argall.

In Argall's writings of 1613, he stated:

> This news much grieved this great king [Wahunsenaca], yet without delay he returned the messenger with this answer, that he desired me to use his daughter well,

> and bring my ship into his river [Pamunkey], and there
> he would give me my demands; which being performed,
> I should deliver him his daughter, and we should be
> friends.[9]

Argall prepared to take sail after receiving Wahunsenaca's answer. While preparing to set sail, he decided to give Japazaw and his wife a copper pot. It was well known that the Powhatan prized copper.[10] The Powhatan attributed spiritual qualities to it. As such, only Powhatan royalty wore copper jewelry; thus it signified a high status in Powhatan society.

Argall used the gift of a copper pot as a means of accusing Japazaw and his wife of betraying Pocahontas for a copper pot. This appears to have been a common tactic of the English colonists.

Captain John Smith had acted similarly when he "traded" for corn. Smith often put his pistol to the head of the chief of a village, forcing him to turn over the village's corn. As Smith left, he would throw down some beads. Later he would tell his fellow colonists that he had traded for the corn.

The long continuation of these implications by popular media[11] and scholars[12] is deeply offensive to Powhatan descendants. It insinuates that the Potowomac valued material possessions over the love and commitment to their relatives and their paramount chief, that they were immoral.[13]

Mattaponi sacred oral history states that before Argall took sail, several of Argall's men returned to Pocahontas's home and killed her husband, Kocoum. They knew the location of Pocahontas's home because they had followed Japazaw's wife when she went to find Pocahontas. Taken by surprise, Kocoum was easily overcome. As the ship pulled out, Pocahontas did not realize her husband had been murdered. Her daughter survived because as Pocahontas left with Japazaw's wife, Ka-Okee[14] was handed over to the other women in tribe.

Instead of going to Werowocomoco to make the exchange, because Wahunsenaca had sent word that he was willing to make the ransom payment, Argall quickly sailed back to Jamestown. Wahunsenaca released the English prisoners, weapons, and tools, as a well as a shipment of corn, fulfilling the ransom demands. Still, the English colonists did not free Pocahontas. Instead, Argall turned Pocahontas over to Sir Thomas Gates at Jamestown. In his 1613 writings, Argall justified his actions, stating that he wanted Gates to settle the ransom details, claiming that he no longer had any obligation in the matter.[14]

Perceiving the reluctance of Wahunsenaca to attack, the English colonists surmised that their best plan would be to keep Pocahontas in a secure area where she could not escape. The English colonists continued to hold any further ransom negotiations at bay while accusing Wahunsenaca of not complying with their demands.

The colonists claimed that holding Pocahontas ensured the peace between the two people; however, the colonists were actually buying more time. They were trying to keep Wahunsenaca from retaliating in response to the colonists driving out and killing the people and destroying the villages and confiscating our crops and farmland all the way up to the falls of the Powhatan River. The English colonists were rapidly bringing in supplies of guns, farming equipment, cattle, other livestock, and immigrants to occupy the land. They were positioning themselves to be strong enough to defend themselves from any major attacks by the Powhatan.

This abduction must have been very hard on Pocahontas. She was only about fifteen to sixteen years old. She must have been frightened. She had been forcibly separated from her husband and child and her father was out of reach. She was on a strange ship, being taken into a strange culture. It had been nearly four years since she had interacted with the English colonists.

Pocahontas's kidnapping was devastating to Wahunsenaca and the Powhatan tribes. It had a tremendous emotional impact on the Powhatan people, who had been friendly to the settlers. They could only hope that the English would not hurt her. All the Powhatan people had a remorseful feeling about it, but her father even more so. The Powhatan felt for him, because he was really down. He would have loved to see her, but he felt that the English colonists were plotting to capture him too. Being the paramount chief, it would have been irresponsible of him to put himself at risk of being taken captive or being assassinated.

Wahunsenaca went into despair over the abduction of Pocahontas. No one could relieve him from his low emotional state. Neither his brothers nor other women could replace his daughter and the affection he had for her. Wahunsenaca sank into deep depression over the kidnapping of Pocahontas.

The English colonists had stolen the Powhatan peace symbol, Pocahontas, Wahunsenaca's beloved daughter.

CHAPTER EIGHT

No Retaliation

The English colonists committed horrendous crimes against the Powhatan people, including raping and enslaving our women and children, as well as kidnapping Pocahontas and murdering her husband. Our land was taken from us and our food was stolen. The Powhatan had once lived in safety and with abundance, yet were now living in fear and starvation. Still, there was no major retaliation by the Powhatan leadership. Chief Japazaw did not retaliate. The paramount chief of the Powhatan nation, Chief Powhatan Wahunsenaca, did not retaliate, neither against the Potowomac tribe nor the English colonists. Pocahontas did not retaliate. Why not?

The answer can be found within the cultural underpinnings of the Powhatan society. A reflection of Powhatan cultural guidelines, which include spiritual principles and principles for proper behavior, gives us examples of why there was no retaliation. Cultural foundations of Powhatan society included respect for life, seeking the good of the tribe, and appeasing evil.[1] Appeasing evil is linked with the concepts of preserving life and seeking the overall good of the community. It involves attempting to strike a balance between submitting to unwanted demands and preventing the loss of life. According to Powhatan philosophy, violent confrontation is never the first desirable choice. Why did Japazaw not fight back? He sought to preserve as much life as possible. Why did Wahunsenaca not retaliate? He sought to protect the life of his beloved daughter, Pocahontas. The *quiakros* (priests) took an opposing position: they advised a swift retaliation against the English colonists after the kidnapping of Pocahontas. They wanted to attempt a rescue of Pocahontas. They perceived the danger that the English's presence posed to the well-being of the whole, the entire Powhatan society. It must be remembered that the *quiakros* had the ultimate power in the Powhatan society. They could have undermined Wahunsenaca's decision not to retaliate, but they choose instead to support his decision. They knew how much Wahunsenaca cared for his daughter Pocahontas.

Why didn't Pocahontas fight or resist? Instead of resisting, Pocahontas bent her will to her captors. She went along with them obediently because there was nothing else she could do. Our belief is that Pocahontas submitted to the English in order to protect her people. If she had behaved badly and resisted the English colonists, they might have taken their anger out on our people. Also, it was the Powhatan custom to respect all life, even the lives of those who sought ill toward our people. Powhatan culture believed in self-respect and maintaining dignity regardless of one's situation. Pocahontas, as the favorite daughter of Wahunsenaca, had been provided superb training. She grew up among the royalty of her culture, so these values had been ingrained in her. Pocahontas would have always carried herself with dignity, whether being held captive by the English colonists or not.

Was Pocahontas afraid? Of course she was. How could she not have been? She had been ripped from her loved ones, separated from her husband, from her small child, from her father, and her friends. Being constantly watched over by the English colonists, she could not have escaped. She was brave, but she must have been terrified.

Pocahontas submitted to the English settlers purely as a means of survival until she could be free. But the English colonists wanted even more from Pocahontas. They wanted to convert her to Christianity. Reflection on Pocahontas's conversion to Christianity while in captivity also reveals aspects of no retaliation.

While Pocahontas was held captive, efforts were made to convert Pocahontas to Christianity and to teach her the English language and English manners. From the English perspective, the Powhatan people were "savages" and "pagans." By English cultural standards, one was not perceived to be a human being if one was not Christian.[2]

Supported by Sir Thomas Dale, Reverend Alexander Whitaker and John Rolfe[3] worked tirelessly to convert Pocahontas to Christianity and to teach her English ways.[4] Pocahontas was continually drilled in the tenets of the Christian faith. Rolfe, an English colonist experimenting with tobacco, volunteered to instruct Pocahontas in the Christian faith. He spent hours with her alone.

Yet Pocahontas did not automatically change her Powhatan ways of behavior. For instance, they had difficulty in keeping her in English clothing. She would pull the English clothes off and the English would have to redress her.

The English colonists were trying to brainwash Pocahontas. They repeatedly told Pocahontas that her father did not love her; otherwise he would have paid the ransom for her return. But due to Pocahontas's superb training and her deep affection for her father, the English colonists were having difficulty in weakening her convictions. So they devised a way to show her that her father did not love her. In the spring of 1614, the English colonists staged an attempt to exchange Pocahontas for Wahunsenaca's ransom payment.* The English colonists in control of Pocahontas had no intention of releasing her. Instead, it was a ploy to prove to her that her father did not love her. Pocahontas was taken to the site for the exchange. The English colonists made demands for corn that the Powhatan were unable to fulfill. It was spring. The majority of the storage of corn for the winter had already been decimated. Opechancanough, who was negotiating for the Powhatan, requested that they be allowed to provide the corn after that year's harvest. This was unacceptable to the English colonists. Shortly afterward, fighting broke out between the English colonists and the Powhatan, ending any

* This was Chief Powahatan Wahunsenaca's second ransom payment.

hopes of an exchange.[5] The colonists used this incident to further prove to Pocahontas that her father coveted English weapons over her.

Shortly after the staged ransom exchange, Pocahontas was converted to Christianity and was baptized.[6] She was given the Christian name Rebecca.[7] Mattaponi sacred oral history tells us very little about Pocahontas's time in captivity, her conversion to Christianity, her baptism and marriage. Was Pocahontas baptized in Jamestown or Henrico? Neither Mattaponi oral history nor scholarship knows.[8] There is no indication that any Powhatan were present during her baptism.[9] It had been about a year since Argall kidnapped her, in April 1613.

Pocahontas's conversion to Christianity raises many questions. Was accepting Christianity a way to survive? Was it a means of trying to appease the English? Did the English brainwash Pocahontas to the point of breaking? Or did Pocahontas accept the new faith as an attempt to look good for her people and in hopes that in return the English would be more lenient to her people? Pocahontas was from Powhatan royalty, so she had a feel for not only representing her people, but also rising above the situation in order to help her people survive. She was smart enough to recognize that the English colonists had weapons and could be dangerous. If she retaliated, the English colonists might hurt her people. Instead of retaliating, she went along with her captors. She was friendly in order to be a good representative for her people.

There are other aspects about Powhatan culture that would have trained Pocahontas to be cooperative. For instance, the stealing of wives and children was a known practice in Powhatan society, as well as within other First American tribes. It occurred between tribes of different languages in their games of war. This was a way to strengthen a tribe's genetic pool. In contrast, the teachings of Christianity opposed such practices, viewing them as forced adultery. Pocahontas would have known that the way to survive and to prolong her life would have been to submit to the circumstances. Pocahontas's adopted mothers trained Pocahontas from an early age on how to behave if she were captured. Later in her life, after the *quiakros* heard that the English colonists were seeking to abduct Pocahontas, the *quiakros* provided her with additional training.

It is hard to say whether Pocahontas truly converted to Christianity or not. Pocahontas may have embraced certain aspects of Christianity, as much of the Christian faith parallels Powhatan spirituality. Comparing the behavior of the Powhatan people to that of the English colonists, it appears that the Powhatan people lived the principles of Christianity more than those who professed faith in it. They offered food to the English colonists. They offered the English colonists a place to live within their society. They taught the English colonists how to farm, fish, and hunt, and how to grow tobacco. The Powhatan people constantly gave to the English colonists. The English colonists constantly took, and they slandered the Powhatan to justify their actions.

Mattaponi sacred oral history does not elaborate on whether Pocahontas truly converted to Christianity or not. In captivity, she was brainwashed. She was captured. She did not know where she was going or what was going to happen to her; thus the best way out was to submit to her captors. However, there may have come a point in her captivity when she did not think she could get out. All of these factors played a part in Pocahontas's decision not to retaliate against her captors. Being a bright person, she would have known what to do to survive the situation.

Euro-American writers and scholars have long claimed that Pocahontas thought her father had deserted her. They have asserted that Pocahontas turned her back on her people and Powhatan ways and embraced the English ways.[10] This is not so.

Pocahontas did not betray her own people. She was ripped from her family against her will. She was not allowed to return. The English colonists told her that her father did not want her because he would not pay her ransom; however, her father was ready and willing to pay the ransom, and more.

Pocahontas's abduction, along with the English's refusal to then release Pocahontas, ensured only a tenuous peace with the Powhatan.

CHAPTER NINE

Marriage in Captivity

The primary reason the English colonists wanted to convert Pocahontas to Christianity was so they could marry Pocahontas to an English colonist named John Rolfe, a widower who was experimenting with growing tobacco. From the English perspective, a person was not considered human unless he or she was a Christian; consequently, Pocahontas would have had to convert to Christianity and be baptized before she could marry an Englishman. There was no possibility that a marriage between a Powhatan and an Englishman would be considered acceptable by English terms without the Powhatan's conversion to Christianity.

Mattaponi sacred oral history does not put a great deal of emphasis on the details of the marriage between Pocahontas and Rolfe, which occurred in the spring of 1614. Instead, the Powhatan were more concerned with Pocahontas's well-being and safety. Among other things, what is known from Mattaponi oral history is that Pocahontas was deeply depressed.

Following Pocahontas's abduction, she sank into a depression. She was not depressed so much from being taken captive. Pocahontas had been trained from the time she was a little girl as to how to deal with such an experience. Being stolen and taken captive was a potential danger for any female Powhatan. But Pocahontas was depressed from being separated from her family, much like her father, who had slipped into depression due to Pocahontas's abduction. The trauma caused by being separated from her husband, son, father, and the rest of her family was enough to bring on Pocahontas's depression. While in captivity at Jamestown, she became fearful and withdrawn. Her condition escalated into what could best be described as having a nervous breakdown. It was so severe that her English captors sent a message to the paramount chief requesting that he send one of

Pocahontas's sisters to stay with her.

Chief Powhatan Wahunsenaca and the *quiakros* (priests) elected to send Mattachanna and her husband, Uttamattamakin, a priest of the highest order and a personal advisor to Pocahontas's father.[1] Mattachanna was Pocahontas's eldest sister by the same mother and had taken over raising Pocahontas when their mother died. The two were very close, and Uttamattamakin was like a wise big brother to Pocahontas. Mattachanna was to care for Pocahontas in her captivity. This gesture was an encouraging sign from the English colonists in that they had expressed concern for Pocahontas's welfare. The Powhatan were grateful for the opportunity to have some contact with Pocahontas, to watch over her and care for her.

When Mattachanna and Uttamattamakin arrived at Jamestown, Pocahontas confided in Mattachanna that she had been raped. Mattaponi sacred oral history is very clear on this: Pocahontas was raped. It is possible that it had been done to her by more than one person and repeatedly. My grandfather and other teachers of Mattaponi oral history[2] said that Pocahontas was raped. The possibility of being taken captive was a danger to beware of in Powhatan society, but rape was not tolerated.

Rape in Powhatan society was virtually unheard of because the punishment for such actions was so severe. Powhatan society did not have prisons. Punishment for wrongful actions often consisted of banishment from the tribe. A man who raped a woman would have been run out of the village, forced to survive on his own or with other outcasts. His family members could have gone out of the village to meet with him, but he could not have returned unless he was able to show sincere remorse by correcting his behavior. Kinship and good relations were highly valued in Powhatan culture, thus banishment was not desirable. In addition, it was difficult to survive alone. Powhatan outcasts often banded together. If the man, or a group of men, continued to be violent, Powhatan warriors would have been sent in to fight them.

While Mattachanna was with Pocahontas, Pocahontas also told her that she believed she was pregnant. Mattachanna found Pocahontas distressed, emotionally disturbed, fatigued, and nauseous.[3] We believe that Mattachanna and Uttamattamakin arrived during the early stages of Pocahontas's pregnancy, in her first trimester. Mattachanna closely monitored Pocahontas. The English colonists who had been involved in taking advantage of Pocahontas took precautions to hide Pocahontas's premarital pregnancy from the other colonists.

Although scholars differ on where Pocahontas stayed during her months of captivity, whether in Jamestown or Henrico, we believe that Pocahontas was moved from Jamestown to Henrico in order to hide her advancing pregnancy. Mattaponi sacred oral history is very clear that Pocahontas was kept in Henrico during the majority of her time in captivity. Pocahontas was taken to live under the supervision of Reverend Alexander Whitaker, who lived upriver at the Henrico plantation located near present-day Richmond.[4] Henrico was more spacious and secluded than Jamestown; thus, fewer colonists would have noticed Pocahontas's pregnancy. In addition, Pocahontas was forced to wear English clothing to conceal her pregnancy.

Pocahontas was not moved to Henrico for security reasons, because Jamestown was the most fortified settlement held by the English colonists. It was here that the colonists stored the majority of their weapons and ammunition. Although a palisade and waterways offered protection to the Henrico plantation, making it difficult for any Powhatan to rescue Pocahontas, Jamestown was even more fortified.

Regardless of any fortification, the reason the Powhatan did not attempt to rescue Pocahontas was due to Wahunsenaca's fear of Pocahontas being hurt if such an attempt were made.

Wahunsenaca's fear was valid in that he had already paid the ransom for Pocahontas and the English colonists had not released her. The lack of the proper response—releasing Pocahontas—indicated the colonists had other agendas in mind. Not knowing their motives, Wahunsenaca did not want to risk Pocahontas being killed. He resorted to the tactic of no retaliation.

Within one year of being held captive, by the spring of 1614 Pocahontas had been converted to Christianity, had been baptized, had given birth to a son of mixed blood, named Thomas, and had been married to the Englishman Rolfe. Mattaponi oral history is adamant that Thomas was born out of wedlock, prior to the marriage ceremony between Pocahontas and Rolfe.

It is not known who Thomas's father was, but one likely candidate appears to be Sir Thomas Dale. Pocahontas became pregnant while in Jamestown, and Dale had access to her there. Scholars William M. S. Rasmussen and Robert S. Tilton acknowledged Dale's close proximity to Pocahontas during her captivity:

> Sir Thomas Dale, the figure with whom she [Pocahontas] is most closely linked after her kidnapping, spent part of his time at Jamestown and part at Henrico, the town he had established in 1611 near the falls of the James [Powhatan] River, and which he had autocratically controlled since.[5]

Assuming Rolfe was not the biological father, this would explain why he named his firstborn son by Pocahontas "Thomas" instead of "John." In addition, Rolfe, the secretary of the colony at the time, did not record the birth of Thomas. Considering that English colonists kept written records, it is odd that there is no record of Thomas Rolfe's birth.[6] It was Rolfe's job to do the census, yet he neglected to record the birth of his own son.

According to Mattaponi sacred oral history, the marriage between Pocahontas and Rolfe occurred at Jamestown. Although Pocahontas obviously submitted to the marriage, it is hard to say whether Pocahontas really loved Rolfe or not. Under the circumstances of Pocahontas's confinement, it is doubtful. The power differential was too great. She was not free to return to her people. She was not free to choose. She married Rolfe because she had just recently had a child by an Englishman. Pocahontas did not understand the motives of the English or what was happening to her; however, she did understand that the English colonists wanted to hide their despicable acts by marrying her to Rolfe and pretending that little Thomas was born after the marriage. She also hoped that her marriage to Rolfe would help create a bond between her people and his, especially after having had a baby by one of them. After all, her father, Wahunsenaca, had wanted the English colonists to be part of the Powhatan nation.

It is equally problematic to discern whether Rolfe loved Pocahontas. In Rolfe's letter to Dale requesting permission to marry Pocahontas, he referred to her as a "creature" instead of using a term to describe a female human being, such as *woman*.[7]

It is significant that this was the first marriage in the "New World" between an English commoner—a tobacco planter—and a member of the Powhatan royal family. Rolfe had much prestige to gain from marrying Pocahontas. Captain John Smith realized the implications of such as a marriage as well. In his 1624 writings, he stated that some may speculate that he could have become a king if he had married Pocahontas; however, Smith noted that he knew better, that marrying Pocahontas would not enable him to become a king.[8] He added that he had never entertained the idea of marrying Pocahontas.[9] Pocahontas was too young at the time Smith was in the colony. She was a child, not yet coming of age into adulthood.[10]

Wahunsenaca gave his permission for the marriage between Pocahontas and Rolfe because Pocahontas was being held captive. His permission was not based on a free choice. If Wahunsenaca refused to grant permission for Pocahontas to marry Rolfe, there was no indication that she could return home. To the contrary, the English colonists holding her may have made her a slave if the marriage was rejected. Dale, on the other hand, was denied permission to marry one of Wahunsenaca's daughters. Although Dale was already married to a woman in England, he had tried to obtain another daughter from Wahunsenaca to marry in the colony. Wahunsenaca had a free choice in that matter. The other daughter was not being held captive. He denied the request.[11]

The English claimed that the wedding between Pocahontas and Rolfe brought peace between the two peoples. But if there was genuine peace, why didn't Pocahontas's father, Wahunsenaca, attend the wedding? The Powhatan custom is that the father gives the bride away, but Wahunsenaca did not do so for Pocahontas. Wahunsenaca loved his daughter dearly and wanted to attend the ceremony but didn't because he feared for his own life. Wahunsenaca had to be very careful that he himself was not captured. He was concerned that the English were hoping to seize him, or possibly kill him, if he came to the wedding. Instead, he sent his brother Opitchapam to attend and observe in his place. There was less chance the English would capture or kill Opitchapam. Although he was Wahunsenaca's brother, technically next in line to be the paramount chief, he was not a strong leader. His demeanor must have been evident to the English colonists as well.

There is no question that at that time, Wahunsenaca had a certain amount of fear of the English colonists. He reasoned, "If you will take my daughter, certainly you would take me." Pocahontas had first come to the English as a sign of peace. Then, later, the English captured the sign of peace. That is like saying to Wahunsenaca, "You are not safe among us."

Wahunsenaca and the *quiakros* recognized that if he were captured, all of the Powhatan people would be immediately subdued, as it would have appeared that their government had been crushed before their eyes. This fear of being taken captive by the English was not simply something Wahunsenaca imagined. His love for his daughter could have overridden that—when you love someone, emotions can override your rational thinking—but a larger issue of the greater good of the Powhatan nation was at stake. The Powhatan thought that if the English colonists captured or killed Wahunsenaca, then there would be no stopping them. Even if they would not have killed him but kept him captive, the rest of the tribes would have been intimidated. They would not have been able to attack those who held their paramount chief. Likewise, Wahunsenaca was unable to call an attack on those who held his favorite daughter. It caused him great heartache that he could not attend his beloved daughter's wedding because of his status as the paramount chief.

Although Wahunsenaca did not attend the wedding, we know through sacred Mattaponi oral history that he gave Pocahontas a pearl necklace as her wedding gift. The pearls were obtained from the Chesapeake Bay oyster beds. The necklace was notable for the large size and fine quality of the pearls. Pearls of this size were rare, making them a suitable gift for a paramount chief's daughter. No mention of this necklace has been found in the English writings, but a portrait of Pocahontas wearing a pearl necklace used to hang in the governor's mansion in Richmond.

Thomas Sully's 1852 painting called *Pocahontas* portrays a Europeanized Pocahontas wearing a pearl necklace. Chief Powhatan Wahunsenaca gave Pocahontas a pearl necklace as her wedding gift. Courtesy of the Virginia Historical Society, Richmond

Thomas Sully's painting *Pocahontas* hung in the governor's mansion in Richmond during George Allen's term as governor of Virginia from 1993 to 1995. This picture of the Cannada family, (left to right) Kathryn "Morning Dove," Nathaniel "Soaring Eagle," Daniel "Lone Wolf," and Brandon "Little Bear," with then-governor George Allen and his wife, was taken during the annual tribute to the Commonwealth of Virginia in compliance to the treaty of 1646 (ratified in 1677).

Sedgeford Hall Portrait by an unidentified artist. Portrait found circa late eighteenth century. Courtesy of the Borough Council of King's Lynn and West Norfolk

A portrait found in the eighteenth century by an unidentified artist, called the *Sedgeford Hall Portrait* supports our oral history. We believe this painting is of Pocahontas and Thomas. The Indian woman depicted is approximately the right age, twenty years old. She has Powhatan facial features. She is wearing a pearl necklace that has pearls of considerable size. Only royal family members would have worn such a prestigious necklace. We believe this is a close likeness of Pocahontas as she would have looked in England. It is possibly the only other known portrait of Pocahontas wearing a pearl necklace. This painting is also unusual because it portrays Pocahontas with Thomas. The child appears to be approximately three years of age and biracial. Thomas would have been close to this age when he was in England with his mother.

CHAPTER TEN

The Colony Saved by the Powhatan

After John Rolfe and Pocahontas were married, the Powhatan *quiakros* (priests) made another attempt to appease the English colonists. The Powhatan *quiakros* became friendlier to the settlers, and especially to Rolfe. The leaders among the English colonists had hoped this would happen. They wanted to capture Pocahontas in order to gain more information on how the Powhatan priests processed tobacco. After his marriage to Pocahontas, Rolfe sought counsel from the Powhatan *quiakros* on curing his tobacco crop.

Rolfe left England to come to the colony in the spring of 1609. His goal was to make a profit growing and processing tobacco. On the way, he was shipwrecked in Bermuda, so Rolfe and his English wife did not arrive at the Jamestown colony until a year later, in the spring of 1610.

Rolfe had been unsuccessful at growing and processing tobacco for nearly three years prior to Pocahontas's kidnapping. The *quiarkros* would not reveal Powhatan knowledge regarding tobacco production to him. Rolfe was becoming frustrated. He knew he would have to become successful soon or the entire economic venture in the "New World" would be in jeopardy.

The year 1616 was the deadline for the initial investments in the Virginia colony.[1] If results were not produced, the authorization from the British royalty as well as the financial backing from individual investors could be withdrawn. Time was running out for the investment company, the Virginia Company of London, to generate returns. The English colony was on the verge of collapsing from lack of financial profit. Rolfe was linked directly with this company. If it withdrew from financing the colony, Rolfe would have to return to England due to the failure of the colony. To a great extent, the English colony's survival depended upon the success of Rolfe's tobacco and/or the public-relations tour in England, which Rolfe and his wife, Pocahontas, were to participate in. The Powhatan people were not aware of the 1616 deadline, but they did know that the colony was failing.

There may have been various reasons that the British Crown chartered the Jamestown colony, perhaps to find a water route to East India or perhaps to prevent the Spaniards from spreading Catholicism throughout the New World.[2] Certainly the reasons of individual colonists varied even more so, such as religious freedom. But ultimately the colony was a business venture sponsored not by the British Crown, but by individuals seeking profitable financial returns. Conditions of this business investment company mandated that such returns would be evident by 1616. The Powhatan, including the *quiakros*, Chief Powhatan Wahunsenaca, and Pocahontas, did not know these details. When they first met, Captain John Smith had told Wahunsenaca that the English were trying to escape from the Spaniards.[3]

One of the first hopes the English had for riches was to find gold. It was believed that Virginia was laden with silver and gold, as the Spaniards had found gold and silver in South America. The immigration to the New World was the English gold rush of the seventeenth century. One motto of the colonists was "No talk, no hope, no work; but dig gold, wash gold, refine gold, load gold."[4] The frenzy for silver and gold often prevailed over level-headedness. The colonists eagerly loaded one ship "with sand that glistened" before Smith could stop them and persuade them to send a cargo of cedar logs back to England instead.[5]

The planned search for gold was one of the reasons the English colonists had not come prepared to be self-sufficient. They came with the intention of obtaining food from the Natives.[6] Their primary objective was to find gold. When gold or other precious metals were not found, they began to try other means of making money, such as glassmaking and timber harvesting. Time was ticking away while one scheme to turn a profit after the next failed. In addition to mining gold and silver, the Spaniards had been successful in growing tobacco. It was only a matter of time before the English colonists undertook the same business enterprise. The Virginia Company of London made arrangements with Rolfe to pursue such an endeavor.

When Rolfe and his English wife arrived in Jamestown in 1610, he immediately focused his attention on growing tobacco. (His wife died sometime later for unknown and undocumented reasons.) By 1612, Rolfe's first crop was curing. It was taller than the Powhatan type of tobacco and showed promise.[7] A few hundred pounds were shipped to England on the *Elizabeth* for trial. The prospect of a successful tobacco industry excited the colonists. They were beginning to have hope in finding a successful means of producing financial returns for the investors in the colony. Late in 1613, after the abduction of Pocahontas, Rolfe received word that his tobacco had begun to be compared favorably with the best Spanish leaf, but it was still not good enough be competitive with the Spanish tobacco. After Rolfe married Pocahontas in the spring of 1614, Sir Thomas Dale gave an extensive tract of land in Henrico to Rolfe.[8]

Rolfe's problems in competing with the Spanish tobacco appeared to stem from lack of knowledge and care in curing the tobacco.[9] According to Mattaponi sacred oral history, the Native people of the New World possessed the knowledge of how to cure and process tobacco successfully. The Spanish gained this knowledge from the Native communities they had subdued.

In the Powhatan society, it was the *quiakros* who possessed the knowledge of how to cure tobacco. Powhatan people planted and tended to the crops, but the *quiakros* cured it.

The Powhatan tobacco was harsher and had a strong bite, making it difficult to inhale deeply. Rolfe used the West Indies tobacco seed, which was much milder to inhale. It was not the objective of the Powhatan to smoke tobacco for pleasure, like the English colonists did. Instead, the Powhatan used tobacco primarily for religious and ceremonial activities. Because of the spiritual quality and reference tobacco had in the Powhatan society, it was the *quiakros* who maintained the knowledge of the final steps of processing it. It was not common knowledge, but knowledge held by the elite. As such, somehow Rolfe needed to access and establish good relations with the Powhatan *quiakros* in order to obtain this Native knowledge.

The solution to Rolfe's challenge to establish good relations with the *quiakros* was to marry Pocahontas. Kinship ties were a very important element in the fabric of Powhatan culture and society. Remember, it was the concept of kinship ties that provided meaning and honor to the obligatory marriages of the Paramount chief and women from the alliance tribes. The purpose of this type of marriage was not for love or a lifetime commitment; instead, it was to build and seal bonds through kinship relations.

Rolfe's problems with tobacco were resolved when the Powhatan *quiakros* accepted Rolfe as their friend because he was married to the paramount chief's daughter. You have to remember, most of the *quiakros* were relatives of Pocahontas. The *quiakros* taught Rolfe Powhatan skills in curing and managing tobacco. They hoped this would satisfy the desires of the English colonists and make them happy so that they would ally themselves with the Powhatan nation. As a result of Rolfe being counseled by the Powhatan *quiakros* as to the best methods of successfully curing tobacco in the New World,[10] Rolfe's tobacco improved to rival any tobacco grown by the Spanish.[11]

In the spring of 1616, a ship named the *Treasurer* set sail for England from the Virginia colony. The voyage was arranged by the Virginia Company of London, which had financed the Jamestown settlement. Samuel Argall, Pocahontas's captor, was the captain of the ship. The primary voyagers were Dale, Rolfe, Pocahontas, and her small son, Thomas.[12] Also on board were nearly a dozen Powhatan,[13] including Mattachanna and Uttamattamakin.[14] Mattachanna cared for Pocahontas, while Uttamattamakin attended to the needs of Rolfe. Other *quiakros* accompanied the voyage in disguise as Powhatan warriors. In order to gain information, the *quiakros* often hid their status from the English colonists by wearing a different type of clothing. The *quiakros* had a distinctive way of dressing, which the English had quickly become aware of and could easily recognize. Although the English colonists never fully grasped the governmental structure of the Powhatan nation, they had recognized the importance of the *quiakros* within the Powhatan society.[15] They considered the *quiakros* a greater threat than the village chiefs. Uttamattamakin, on the other hand, openly conversed among the English colonists as a Powhatan priest. While in England, he openly criticized the English colonists.[16]

The primary cargo on this voyage consisted of Rolfe's tobacco. The success of the tobacco, cured with the help of the Powhatan, was the English colonists' last chance to save the colony financially. In a letter to England prior to their departure, Dale described the crop as "exceedingly good tobacco."[17] It was a critical time for the English colony, but Dale, Argall, and Rolfe—prominent men in the Jamestown colony—were returning to England with a load of promising tobacco and Wahunsenaca's daughter. The voyage conveyed to the royalty in England—and perhaps to the colonists as well—the impression that all was well between the Powhatan people and the English colonists.

Upon their arrival in England, Rolfe's tobacco—which had been grown on the Powhatan land with the help of the Powhatan *quiakros*—surpassed the taste and flavor of the Spanish tobacco. It was a success. The Virginia Company quickly assessed the profitability of tobacco in the new colony. Refinancing the

Virginia colony would come easily now. With financial worries eased, the presence of Pocahontas, the daughter of Wahunsenaca, was even more of a festive occasion. To England, all must have seemed well with the development of the English colony.

The Powhatan actually saved the colony by sharing their knowledge of tobacco curing and management. This sharing of knowledge was directly linked to Wahunsenaca and his daughter, Pocahontas. It was directly related to Wahunsenaca because he had wanted to be friends, at peace, in alliance with the English from the beginning. This provided another opportunity to try to make that agenda work. It was related directly to Pocahontas because she was held in such high favor because of her father, who was the paramount chief. She was married to Rolfe, the English colonist interested in growing tobacco. In addition, many of the *quiakros* were relatives of Pocahontas. If they could, the *quiakros* wanted to make a good relationship out of the devastating events that had occurred. Both the actions taken by individuals and underlining Powhatan cultural persuasions were in play, affecting the responses and actions of the people involved. The deep parental affection Wahunsenaca had for his daughter is always evident throughout Mattaponi sacred oral history.

However, the efforts of the Powhatan *quiakros* had the opposite effects they had hoped for. Instead of the English colonists embracing the Powhatan people and becoming their allies, the colonists' greed was unleashed. Settlers in Jamestown and the surrounding plantations rushed to obtain more Powhatan land to grow tobacco. To a great extent, the search for gold was forgotten. Tobacco became like gold to the English colonists. It eventually became a form of currency in the Virginia colony.[18] Settlers extended the boundaries of their communities by grabbing the already cleared land of the Powhatan to grow their own tobacco. It was difficult to clear huge trees—the tree logs, the tree limbs, tree stumps, and roots—then prepare the soil to make it suitable to grow tobacco plants. This would have taken the colonists many years; the colonists did not want to wait. So they coveted the Powhatan tribes' open, fertile fields even more so. The English colonists took more and more Powhatan land by force, killing and enslaving larger numbers of Powhatan people. Tobacco was so profitable, every little bit of open space was used to plant it. It was also so profitable that Dale passed a mandate that required every farmer to grow enough corn for subsistence instead of only growing tobacco.[19]

CHAPTER ELEVEN

Pocahontas's Revelation

Traveling to England with Captain Samuel Argall might have caused Pocahontas to reflect on the events in her recent past. The voyage provided her with long days of idle time. Prior to this trip, time had been moving very quickly for Pocahontas. Unexpected changes of significant proportion had occurred in her life in a relatively short period of time. There had been only one year between the time she was kidnapped, in the spring of 1613, and baptized, converted to Christianity, and married to Rolfe in the spring of 1614. Being on the same ship with the same captain in a new stressful experience of crossing the Atlantic Ocean could have reminded Pocahontas of being taken captive on the banks of the Potomac River, being torn away from her husband, Kocoum, and her young daughter, Ka-Okee.

Although the financial investors in the Virginia Company were very important to the continuance of the English colony, these were not the only people in England the investment company had to appease. They also had to placate the royalty of England and the Church. The English colonists wanted to take Pocahontas to England to show her off to the King and Queen of England, as well as to the Church of England, to give the impression that relations were good between the colonists and the Powhatan tribes. In addition, there were people in England who did not approve of the Native people having been mistreated. There was a possibility that support, including financial, moral, and support from royal charters, might have been withdrawn if it were known how the leaders of the colony were actually treating the Powhatan people

The leaders in the English colony used Chief Powhatan Wahunsenaca's daughter Pocahontas to make it appear to England that Wahunsenaca, king of the Powhatan nation, and all of its leaders approved of Pocahontas's marriage to Rolfe. In reality, Pocahontas had been kidnapped. Leaders within the Virginia colony had refused to accept Wahunsenaca's ransom. The colonists did not recognize Pocahontas's marriage to Kocoum; they considered it to be pagan. Neither did they acknowledge her son by this marriage. The colonists believed it would be good for Pocahontas to convert to Christianity—or at least appear to do so—and to remarry. Then they could take her to England to "promote the goodwill of her people." The presence of Pocahontas in England camouflaged the brutal treatment of the Powhatan people. In reality, the leaders in the English colony were using Pocahontas to try to gain the support of the people in England for the colony and its expansion so that the new colony would not fail.

The Virginia Company took Pocahontas to England to show her off. She was intelligent and bright, Christianized, and of Powhatan royal lineage. They thought investors would see in Pocahontas that the Powhatan people could be "civilized." Pocahontas would have eased their fears of the rumors that the Powhatan people were murdering savages, as well as dispel the stories that the Powhatan people were being mistreated by the colonists. Also, Pocahontas's presence in England would convey the conception that Wahunsenaca supported the Virginia Company's efforts, that the Powhatan people and the colonists had an excellent rapport, and that the Powhatan were anxious to be Christianized.

Pocahontas was unaware of the fact that the trip to England was a scheme to raise money for the Virginia Company, to finance even more Europeans to come with their weapons to her homeland to kill her people and take their land.

The *quiakros* (priests) did not know the real motivation for taking Pocahontas to England in 1616 either. However, many of them, particularly Uttamattamakin, had advised Wahunsenaca to take measures to prevent Pocahontas from going to England. They had recommended a covert operation, such as sending in warriors to rescue her before the ship departed. Again, Wahunsenaca feared for the life of his daughter, tried to appease evil, and did not retaliate.

While in England, Pocahontas was treated like royalty among the British elite. The British Crown greeted her warmly. Pocahontas was dressed in English attire. She was taught English customs and etiquette, which must have dignified her in the eyes of the Queen.

Mattachanna had in-depth talks with Pocahontas during the voyage and while in England, and accompanied Pocahontas everywhere she went, except perhaps when Pocahontas was visiting with dignitaries.

Mattachanna had Pocahontas's pulse. She understood and knew Pocahontas's innermost feelings. This is how we learned the history of what happened to Pocahontas in England: Mattachanna and Uttamattamakin reported back to Wahunsenaca upon their return. That is how we know Pocahontas did not betray her people.

In time, Pocahontas recognized what her presence in England really meant. She realized she was being used as a showpiece for her husband, his partners, and the Virginia Company in an effort to gain additional financial support from England. Pocahontas did not perceive the extent to which the colonist businessmen had betrayed her and her people until she reached England. When Captain John Smith was made a *werowance* (chief) at Werowocomoco, he had pledged his allegiance to Wahunsenaca. It was inconceivable to Wahunsenaca and Pocahontas that Smith would deceive and betray them.

Our people could not conceive of deception because their word was a bond of law. Betrayal never entered our minds: when you blow tobacco smoke from a pipe to the four winds, to Ahone, the Good and Great Spirit, your word is good. You do not break your word, which is sacred. We could not conceive of people not adhering to their word.

Imagine how Pocahontas must have felt when she discovered that Smith was still alive, as well as that he had betrayed her, her father, and her people! Smith had lied to her father, making Wahunsenaca feel that he and the English colonists were coming under the Powhatan nation. When Wahunsenaca asked Smith what they were doing on their land, what they wanted, Smith never answered him truthfully. Smith had deceived the Powhatan from the beginning. He had told Wahunsenaca that the Spaniards had defeated the English and they needed time to recover. In England, Pocahontas at last understood the reality of the true intentions of the English colonists. Pocahontas knew she had to see Smith before she left England, to confront him about his deceit of her father. Pocahontas wanted to tell Smith these things as best she could in his language, English.

Pocahontas met with Smith outside of London, in Middlesex. At their reunion, Pocahontas was enraged at Smith.[1] She was angry not because he had left her without saying good-bye or without giving her an explanation or because she had been the "slighted lover," as has been portrayed by popular stories. Pocahontas's fury toward Smith was because of his betrayal to her people. Wahunsenaca and the Powhatan people had offered their hand in friendship to the English colonists. Smith, the leader of the colony, had personally deceived them. He had given his pledge to be the English *werowance* and to bring the English colonists into alliance with the Powhatan nation. In England, Pocahontas finally realized that Smith had betrayed her father's trust, and her people were going to suffer terribly because of it.

With growing horror, Pocahontas realized the extent of the true intentions of the English. She longed even more to go back to her homeland. She dearly missed her father, she desired to show her father her young son, Thomas, and to see her daughter, Ka-Okee.

CHAPTER TWELVE

Murder in England

Arrangements were made to return to Virginia in the spring of 1617. Again, Samuel Argall was the captain of the ship. As the *Treasurer* began to make its way toward the open ocean, Pocahontas and John Rolfe dined with Argall in the captain's chamber. Pocahontas quickly became ill. She returned to her quarters by herself, sick to her stomach, and vomited. She told Mattachanna that the English must have put something in her food. Mattachana and Uttamattamakin tried to care for Pocahontas in her sudden illness. As Pocahontas began to convulse, Mattachanna went to get Rolfe. When they returned, Pocahontas had died.

Pocahontas had died! Rolfe immediately told Argall to take Pocahontas's body and their son, Thomas, to Gravesend, England. It had the closest available churchyard in which to bury her. The clergy could keep Thomas until Rolfe's English relatives arrived to take Thomas home with them. Rolfe wanted to return to Virginia as quickly as possible, and the ship departed immediately.[1] Pocahontas was buried in Gravesend, and Rolfe abandoned little Thomas in England in the care of relatives while he returned to Virginia to proceed with his tobacco business and help fulfill England's plans to destroy the Powhatan nation.

Upon returning from England, Mattachanna and the high priest Uttamattamakin, together with other *quiakros* (priests) who had accompanied them on the journey, reported to Chief Powhatan Wahunsenaca that Pocahontas had been murdered in England. The *quiakros* reported that Pocahontas was most likely poisoned. Pocahontas was in good health while in England and when she got on the boat to head home. They were still on the river, not yet having reached the open sea, when Pocahontas got sick. After coming from the captain's cabin, Pocahontas had a radical problem and died. This is the account of the Mattaponi sacred oral history.

Some scholars have conjectured that Pocahontas died of tuberculosis; however, tuberculosis does not strike quickly. Chronic tuberculosis lasts for a long time. Even acute tuberculosis does not kill that quickly. There would have been numerous signs if Pocahontas had had tuberculosis. Yet she was in good health when she got on the ship. She was elated and excited to be returning to her homeland.

Upon learning the truth of the intentions of the English during her visit to England, Pocahontas became emboldened. No longer were her eyes closed to their deceit.

We believe that the English colonists did not want Pocahontas to return to her homeland. Being away from her father for so long, the first thing she would have done would have been to run to him. She would have wanted to reveal Smith's deceptions. Also, Pocahontas was anxious to show her son Thomas to her father, as well as see her firstborn son. Pocahontas wanted to return to her homeland. She loved her father and longed to see him. Rolfe and his cohorts knew that. In the beginning, when she was first captured, she had been led to believe by Rolfe and others that her father neither loved her nor wanted her back. They told Pocahontas that her father had refused to pay her ransom and had abandoned her. In England, she saw through their lies.

By then, Rolfe and the Virginia Company associates ascertained that Pocahontas knew that Smith had lied to her father and that some English businessmen were behind a scheme to remove her father from his throne and take the land from the Powhatan people. This justified the decision by the English colonists not to take Pocahontas back to her homeland. They knew that she would slip away as soon as she had a chance to do so and that she would take Thomas. Certain people believed that Pocahontas would endanger the English settlement, especially because she had new insights into the political strategy of the English colonists to break down the Powhatan structure, so they plotted to murder her.

The murder of Pocahontas raises some serious questions. Was Pocahontas's kidnapping, her conversion to Christianity, her marriage to Rolfe, and her murder all planned at once, long before the tragic events took place? Or were the individual events planned independently or perhaps as a result of each other? Or was it a partial combination thereof? Mattaponi sacred oral history suggests that the plots to kidnap and murder Pocahontas were conceived long before the events occurred. One role of the *quiakros* was to act as intelligence agents. They were constantly gathering information about what was happening that pertained to the safety of the Powhatan nation. As such, Mattaponi sacred oral history suggests that Pocahontas's death was planned prior to Argall's ship leaving for England. The *quiakros* had warned Wahunsenaca prior to Pocahontas's departure that she might not return. They had advised him to send in warriors to rescue her. Wahunsenaca feared Pocahontas would be harmed in such an attempt, and thus did not cede to the advice of the *quiakros*. If this is so, Pocahontas's revelation in England did not directly determine her murder, but it probably would have provided further justification for it to those who were plotting her demise.

Who was behind Pocahontas's murder? Did one or more than one person conceive this plot? If the plan was devised prior to leaving for England, the probable suspects would include Rolfe, Argall, and Sir Thomas Dale. Even Reverend Alexander Whitaker could have been involved.

Scholars have indicated that Dale, Rolfe, and Whitaker had close ties to each other.[2] All three had major roles in what happened in Pocahontas's life after she was abducted. Dale eventually took custody of Pocahontas after Argall took her to Jamestown. Whitaker maintained Pocahontas's house arrest and surveillance.

All three sought to convert Pocahontas to Christianity. Rolfe married Pocahontas. Dale provided a large tract of land for Rolfe to grow tobacco. A Dale-Rolfe-Whitaker trio comprising agreements and pacts is not out of the realm of possibility, but Mattaponi sacred oral history does not reveal who or how many persons were behind her murder.

We believe it is most likely that more than one person was involved. It is doubtful that the King and Queen of England were informed, because we believe they would have tried to protect the Powhatan people if they had known what was actually happening in the colony. But they were too far away and they could not control the situation from across the sea. Instead, many colonists, particularly those involved with the Virginia Company, were gaining undue power in Pocahontas's homeland. Greed in combination with a surge of newly found power overrode efforts of the British Crown to work peacefully and respectfully with the Powhatan nation. Some men who had not held elite status in England carved out enormous power for themselves in the English settlement. It is possible that British royalty was unaware of the liberties their subjects were taking in Virginia among the Powhatan people.

Why did Pocahontas die so suddenly at such a young age? Longevity was the norm in Powhatan society. The Powhatan were people of the ecosystem. The foods they ate were healthy, low in cholesterol, and high in nutrients. Although he was advanced in years, Wahunsenaca was healthy and strong. Smith described Wahunsenaca as being tall, well proportioned, and having a "very able and hardy body to endure any labor."[3]

Wahunsenaca was in good physical health until the abduction of Pocahontas. Grief over the loss of his daughter caused Wahunsenaca to sink even further into depression. He had not accepted the advice of the *quiakros* to swiftly attack and attempt to recover Pocahontas. Instead, he had always held onto a thread of hope that she would come home. His hope was now smashed. A self-blame came over him: "If I had attacked, if I had tried to save her, if she had been killed on our soil, then at least she would have died on our soil. I would have been able to see her body."

Pocahontas's murder was hard for Wahunsenaca to accept. It was an overpowering grief for him, and he cast blame on himself. He had already been concerned about Pocahontas's well-being and whether he was making the right decisions or not when the English colonists took her to England and the *quiakros* advised Wahunsenaca not to allow her to go, though the *quiakros* felt not that the English were going to kill her, but that they were not going to let her come back.

Wahunsenaca's depression over Pocahontas's death led to his demise. He could no longer make competent decisions. The *quiakros* had to basically relieve him of his duties. The *quiakros* eventually took Wahunsenaca to his brother Opechancanough. At that time, upon the advice of the *quiakros*, Wahunsenaca agreed to turn the position of being the paramount chief over to his brother, Opechancanough. The *quiakros* normally would have chosen the next eldest brother; however, Opitchapam, who was older than Opechancanough, was not a leader of any kind. He was weak and lacked leadership ability.[4] Wahunsenaca had been a leader who tried to work things out with diplomacy. He was called a "peace chief." The *quiakros* believed the time had come for a different approach. Opechancanough was more of a warrior who would stand up and defend his country. He was called a "war chief."

When the position of paramount chief went to Opechan-conough, the capital was moved over to the Pamunkey region along the Pamunkey (York) River. These recent events—the kidnapping of Pocahontas, the depression of Wahunsenaca, together with the rapid influx of more and more colonists, which increased the killing of Powhatan people for fertile land—contributed to the start of the rapid decline of the Powhatan nation. There was no way to change these circumstances. Due to the aggressiveness of the English settlers, the Powhatan capital remained in the Pamunkey region.

Wahunsenaca died in the spring of 1618, within a year of Pocahontas's death. He died blaming himself for Pocahontas's death. He died blaming himself for letting his beloved wife down. "Take care of my child for me," were her last words to him as she died giving birth to Pocahontas. Wahunsenaca died of a broken heart. Pocahontas, the Powhatan peace symbol, had been murdered.

In the Years That Followed

Chief Powhatan Wahunsenaca

Chief Powhatan Wahunsenaca died in April 1618. It had been less than a year since Pocahontas's death. His final resting place is in a mound on the Pamunkey reservation approximately ten miles from the Mattaponi reservation, where the *quiakros* (priests) resided. The two reservations are approximately fifteen miles outside of West Point, Virginia.

Pocahontas

Pocahontas was less than twenty-one years old at the time of her death. She was buried in the vault beneath the chancel of Saint George's Church in Gravesend, England. Church records give the date of burial as March 21, 1617.

The original Saint George's Church was destroyed by fire on August 24, 1727. Later it was rebuilt. Sadly, during the reconstruction, the burial site was greatly disturbed and the human remains of various persons were intermixed. Pocahontas's grave proper was demolished.

The Powhatan people have been unsuccessful in their attempts to have Pocahontas's remains returned to her homeland. We believe she would want to be buried in Virginia, beside her beloved father, Chief Powhatan Wahunsenaca.

Kocoum

We believe that Pocahontas's husband Kocoum was killed by the English after Pocahontas was kidnapped. Mattaponi oral history tells us that the English killed Kocoum prior to Captain Samuel Argall's departure for Jamestown with Pocahontas aboard ship. The British did not recognize the marriage of Pocahontas and Kocoum, believing it to be pagan. Ka-Okee, the daughter of Pocahontas and her warrior husband, survived. Some of his descendants live today. Among them are a famous entertainer Wayne Newton and the Newton family.

Captain John Smith

Captain John Smith's final meeting with Pocahontas outside of London does much to confirm his failed relations with the royal family of England and British aristocrats. Smith never returned to Pocahontas's homeland in the "New World." Mattaponi oral history implies that the close relationship Smith established with Chief Powhatan Wahunsenaca as the *werowance* (chief) of the English may have created envy and jealousy among other colonists. It is possible that powerful people within the Virginia Company wanted Smith expelled so that they could gain power over the Powhatan nation instead.

Smith's accounts of the events surrounding Pocahontas allegedly saving his life were written years after her death. At that time, there was no one to attest to what he had written. In addition, the 1624 publication of these writings occurred two years after the 1622 Powhatan insurrection. This one-day attack shocked the English colonists. As a result, the English swore that they would never make peace with the Powhatan.[1]

Smith was never substantially rewarded for his service to the colony—the Virginia Company ignored his requests for reward monies. Smith died, unmarried, on June 21, 1631, in England. He was buried in London.[2]

The Powhatan People Who Sailed aboard the *Treasurer* in 1616

A dozen or more Powhatan, including Mattachanna and Uttamattamakin, accompanied Pocahontas to England in 1616.[3] What happened to these Powhatan? Mattaponi oral history holds that more than half of the Powhatan people who accompanied Pocahontas to England in 1616 were immediately sold as either servants or as creatures to be displayed in cages in carnivals. If they tried to retaliate against the harsh treatment or if a female servant became pregnant after being raped, they were taken to Bermuda, then sold into slavery. Pocahontas's oldest sister, Mattachanna, and Powhatan's priestly advisor Uttamattamakin returned to their homeland. They provided Chief Powhatan Wahunsenaca and the *quiakros* (priests) with the knowledge and information they had gathered and experienced there. This is how we know that Pocahontas did not betray her people. This is the foundation of our oral history on Pocahontas that we have carried for nearly 400 years within the Mattaponi Indian reservation.

Captain Samuel Argall

In 1617, Captain Samuel Argall was appointed deputy governor and admiral of Virginia.[4] He was later knighted.[5] He returned to Virginia, where he continued to exploit the Powhatan for his own financial gain. He died in 1639.[6]

John Rolfe

Upon John Rolfe's return to Virginia in 1617 after the death of Pocahontas, Rolfe quickly married Jane Pierce, an English widow, his third marriage. [7] He became a major landowner in the "New World."[8]

Although the English asserted in their writings that they survived in spite of attacks by the Powhatan, there is no question that the Powhatan did not seriously attack the English colonists until 1622. We believe Rolfe died during this one-day attack by the Powhatan. This attack had a devastating effect on the English colonists. As a result, they became relentless in trying to destroy the Powhatan.

Outside the descendant Powhatan tribes, little thought has been given to the fact that the Powhatan did not retaliate against the English colonists until 1622, fifteen years after the first English ships arrived in 1607. Enduring patience in order to determine justly another's intent was one of the characteristics of the Powhatan society.

Sir Thomas Dale

Sacred Mattaponi oral history indicates that the English colonists raped Pocahontas while she was in captivity and that Thomas Rolfe was born prior to the wedding between Pocahontas and John Rolfe. It has often been assumed that Rolfe was the culprit, but after collaborating on this book, the authors question whether Sir Thomas Dale might have been the biological father of Pocahontas's son Thomas. Pochahontas's son bore the same name as Dale—Thomas, not John. As a leading figure in the colony at that time, Dale would have had the opportunity and ability to access Pocahontas. Plus, although he was already married (with a wife in England), Dale had requested to marry another daughter of Chief Powhatan Wahunsenaca, and Wahunsenaca had refused.

Rolfe's actions also lend credence to the possibility of Dale being the biological father of Thomas. Although he was the secretary of the colony from 1614 to 1616,[9] Rolfe failed to record the date of Thomas's birth. After Pocahontas's death, he abandoned Thomas to relatives in England.

In 1619, Dale sickened and died in the East Indies.

Thomas Rolfe

Tragically, after his mother's death, Thomas Rolfe was abandoned in England in a strange culture among strange relations. Thomas grew up and was educated in England. He did not return to Virginia until he was an adult, sometime after his father died. When he finally arrived in Virginia, Thomas settled on his father's land in Surry. Thomas married and had many descendants. Among them are some of the foremost families of Virginia.

Chief Werowance Opechancanough

It was another four years after the death of Chief Powhatan Wahunsenaca before Chief Werowance Opechancanough led a full outright attack on the English in 1622 in an attempt to preserve the Powhatan society. The Powhatan viewed the attack as an act of survival.

After the success of Rolfe's tobacco, more and more settlers poured into the Powhatan territory, killing the Powhatan in order to seize more Powhatan lands. The increase in the colonist population reached a crisis point for the Powhatan, causing Opechancanough to say, "We are going to have to push them out before they kill us all!" Nearly a third of the English population in the Virginia colony was wiped out in one day. However, the violent resistance of the Powhatan did not discourage the English. Instead, they became enraged with the desire for revenge. The Powhatan attack in 1622 justified the indiscriminate killing of the Powhatan by the English for years to come.

The English quickly replenished their population after the 1622 attack. Within two years, a 1624 census listed 1,275 persons living in Virginia. In 1644, Opechancanough reiterated his belief that if the English were not stopped, the Powhatan would perish. Although more than ninety years old and in ill health, Opechancanough led another major attack on the English colonists. This time, Opechancanough was captured. He was shot in the back, murdered in his jail cell by his English guard.

The Powhatan and the English colonists agreed upon a peace treaty in 1646.

Tobacco

Gold or other precious metals had not been discovered in Virginia. Efforts by the English to find a highly profitable commodity had failed. The colonists had to find a way to make the new colony financially profitable. Most had come to the "New World" seeking fortunes. Well-educated John Rolfe had a plan to gain prosperity by growing and exporting tobacco, as the Spanish colonists were doing in the Caribbean Islands. If the colony failed, his aspirations would sink along with it. It was Rolfe's success with tobacco that turned the tide for the Virginia colonists and provided the Virginia colony with a reason for being.[10] The 1616 deadline for the English colony to produce financial returns on their investments weighed heavily on the minds of the leaders of the English colony. The primary objective was to obtain large financial gains in the Virginia colony venture.

In 1612, only two years after he arrived in Jamestown, Rolfe's first crop of tobacco was curing in Jamestown. It was taller than the Powhatan type of tobacco. A few hundred pounds of Rolfe's first crop were shipped to England on the *Elizabeth* for trial. It showed promise.[11] The prospects of tobacco excited the colonists.

Late in 1613, Rolfe received word that his tobacco had begun to be compared favorably with the best Spanish leaf, though it commanded a price slightly lower than Spanish-grown tobacco. His problems appeared to stem from lack of knowledge and care with curing the new strains of tobacco, as well as poor crop management.[12]

Sometime after their arrival in Jamestown, Rolfe's wife died.[13] Rolfe met Pocahontas while she was being held in captivity. Along with Sir Thomas Dale and Reverend Alexander Whitaker, Rolfe instructed Pocahontas in the doctrines of Christianity. Within a year of Pocahontas having been taken captive, Rolfe married Pocahontas, in the spring of 1614.[14] Rolfe was then counseled by the Powhatan as to the best methods for successfully growing tobacco in the New World.[15] His tobacco improved, rivaling any grown by the Spanish.[16]

Growing tobacco required a lot of cleared land. The forests were full of virgin trees. Trees were very large in Virginia at that time. Clearing the land was difficult work, even for the colonists, who had metal tools. In addition, after clearing away the trees and tree stumps, the soil needed to be prepared. The Powhatan *quiakros* (priests) were experts at tending the soil and creating fertile farmlands. The colonists wanted the Powhatan land that was already cleared, because they thought it took too long to prepare wilderness land. So, instead of clearing land themselves, the colonists attacked and killed Powhatan villagers, especially those who lived along the Powhatan (James) River, in order to confiscate the lands they had cleared for their crops. Colonists in the New World focused on clearing land to develop new fields to grow more tobacco.

From 1615 to 1616, about 2,500 pounds of tobacco were shipped to England. By 1617, exports of Virginia tobacco to England totaled 20,000 pounds. In 1618, exports doubled. Twelve years later, 1.5 million pounds of tobacco were shipped from Virginia.[17]

Prior to the success of tobacco, the English colony had not been able to develop an economical means of paying back its investors. The year 1616 was the year the investors in the Virginia Company were to receive their returns, otherwise the colony would fold. It was a critical time for the colony. The number of new investors was low. The English colony was on the brink of collapsing. If tobacco had not been successful, the English colony would have folded.

Tobacco became the gold the colonists had been looking for. The Powhatan provided them with the missing element to make it successful.

Contemporary Powhatan descendants Kathryn "Morning Dove" Cannada and her sons, (left) Nathaniel "Soaring Eagle" and (right) Daniel "Lone Wolf," dressed in regalia.

Pa-naw (Farewell)

The Other Side of History

The inclusion of oral tradition within anthropological work has a long and distinguished history. The very genesis of the discipline's ethnographic work is rooted in the descriptive accounts of conversations between researchers and Native people. Anthropologists sought to obtain accurate information from knowledgeable individuals who had the authority to speak on specific topics by interviewing individuals who were charged with "keeping" stories for their communities. These interviews helped anthropologists gain insight into other people's worldviews as well as alternative versions of history.

In the early twentieth century, a significant amount of ethnographic work focused on first-person accounts or narratives compiled from conversations with prominent Native leaders or famous Indian warriors. These narratives were gathered in the late nineteenth century during what was believed to be the "last days of the vanishing Indian." Other anthropological works of the period sought to gain a more complete picture of traditional lifeways by gathering data on a wide array of traditional Native practices. Interestingly, during the early decades of the twentieth century, a number of these publications found an enthusiastic audience among general readers who were enthralled by the subject matter and drawn to the biographical component of the work. Over time, this historical and particularistic approach to anthropological fieldwork declined in popularity.

Today, anthropology is oriented toward more theoretically focused research, which seeks to answer questions about such topics as culture change, identity formation, and the impact the colonial encounter had on indigenous communities. However, individuals interested in collecting the oral histories of individuals and communities continue to contribute in important ways to the fields of anthropology and history. Currently, there is renewed interest in the collection and documentation of oral traditions that can give us insight into Native-centered and alternative perspectives on historical events. With this renewed interest in oral history comes a renewed focus on the methodological approaches to oral history and a concern with the processes that result in the creation and maintenance of these traditions.

America is a place with few overarching national narratives and even fewer oral traditions. However, we can all agree that one story that is writ large in our national memory is the story of the young Powhatan woman known to us as Pocahontas. Rarely do we consider that what we know about Pocahontas may represent only one version of her life story. Until recently, nearly all published accounts of Pocahontas were crafted by non-Native scholars. Even though the Pocahontas narrative is deeply intertwined with the identity and history the Powhatan people, their perspectives on the seventeenth-century events that are so central to their own histories rarely appeared in print. Perhaps the time was not right to do so until now.

Dr. Linwood "Little Bear" Custalow is well known in Virginia's Native and non-Native community as a physician and the eldest son of the late Chief Daniel Webster "Little Eagle" Custalow of the Mattaponi tribe in King William County, Virginia. Custalow wears the mantle of Mattaponi tribal historian with humility and a deep sense of responsibility to his tribal community. His decision to share this material with a non-Native audience at this time comes after much reflection. During the past several years, Angela L. Daniel has worked closely with Custalow to document and edit this Mattaponi version of Pocahontas's life and legacy. Daniel interviewed Custalow weekly, giving careful attention to methodological concerns and creating a detailed transcription of interviews with Custalow, which was the basis for this book.

This provocative account of the life of Pocahontas challenges us and our notions of the "facts" of history. Some may denounce what is claimed by Custalow while others will support this version as the "true story." No doubt questions will emerge after the reading of this book. Some readers may ask, "Why now? Why share this story now?" Others will ask, "Is this version the true story, and how will scholars receive this work?" A more important question might be, "How would this Mattaponi version of history have been received if it had been shared with the non-Native community at some other point in the past?" Most important of all, is there room for alternate versions of history, or must we keep Pocahontas on the other side of history?

—Danielle Moretti-Langholtz, PhD,
Department of Anthropology,
College of William & Mary,
Williamsburg, Virginia

ACKNOWLEDGMENTS

Especially from Dr. Linwood "Little Bear" Custalow

I am beholden to my family, who was extremely helpful and supportive. Especially to my wife, Barbara, who wanted so much to see this book in print and who supported my endeavors in any way she could. I wish to express my profound gratitude also to my brother Chief Carl "Lone Eagle" Custalow for endorsing our portrayal of Pocahontas and to Pocahontas's father, the great Chief Powhatan Wahunsenaca. To my sisters Shirley "Little Dove" Custalow McGowan, Edith "White Feather" Custalow Kuhns, and Debbie "White Dove" Custalow Porreco and my brother Leon "Two Feathers" Custalow, I thank you for your unfailing support and encouragement. Thank-you also to my sisters Eleanor "Pocahontas" Cannada and Delores "Little White Dove" Salmons and my brother Ryland "Running Deer" Custalow.

Thank-you to Dr. Patricia Ferguson Walkinson, archivist at the Library of Virginia, for her extraordinary professional support. I wish to thank Ruth Salzberg, author and friend, for her gracious assistance and critical help with the manuscript.

Thank-you as well to Robert Haigh, who proofread our manuscript. Special thanks to my right hand, Angela L. Daniel "Silver Star." Without her general all-around genius and inherent sunny disposition, writing this book would not have been so enjoyable. Special thanks to Marjorie "Sunflower" Sargent, who with persistence and dedication saw us through to the final manuscript you now hold in your hands. Without her, this book may not have been born.

Thanks to my grandfather Chief George "Thundercloud" F. Custalow for allowing me to be his favorite grandson and for his faith in me to be the caretaker of the Mattaponi history. And thanks to my uncle Chief Otha T. (O. T.) Custalow, who helped me fill in the gaps of the Mattaponi history, especially after my grandfather's passing.

Last but not least, I am blessed to have had Chief Daniel Webster "Little Eagle" Custalow as my father. Talking to him over the years has changed my thinking and my writing. My father passed away a year before we began working on *The True Story of Pocahontas*. He was a remarkable and loving father who gave more to this book than anyone else and whom I will always miss. I will never forget all that he taught me and all he brought into my life by inviting me into his. He fills my heart.

—Dr. Linwood "Little Bear" Custalow

Especially from Angela L. Daniel "Silver Star"

I am grateful to Mattaponi tribal members, the University of Virginia, the College of William & Mary, loved ones, and family members.

I have been raised by the Mattaponi. In 2000, the late Chief Daniel Webster "Little Eagle" Custalow honored me with the Indian name "Silver Star." Numerous Mattaponi tribal members have supported my efforts to acquire a higher education and learn their ways of life. The late Chief Daniel Webster's daughters and sons, including Shirley "Little Dove" Custalow McGowan and Edith "White Feather" Custalow Kuhns, Carl "Lone Eagle" Custalow, and Dr. Linwood "Little Bear" Custalow, as well as other tribal members and their families, have welcomed me with warmth. The current Mattaponi chief Carl "Lone Eagle" Custalow provided recommendations for me to both the University of Virginia and the College of William & Mary.

At the University of Virginia (UVA), my deepest gratitude extends to Professor Edith Turner, who believed in me as an undergraduate and affirmed me as a fellow anthropologist. Her encouragement later withstood the criticism of those who denied my identity as anthropologist due to this work. I owe Professor Emeritus Jeffrey Hopkins a tremendous debt for sponsoring me as a graduate student in the Religious Studies Department at UVA. The promise of a scholarship was withdrawn from an anthropology department after I revealed that the Mattaponi oral history posed a contradictory position. The assistance and support from Professors Karen Lang and Charles Marsh enabled me to earn a master's degree at UVA. They provided a positive experiential base, demonstrating that earning a degree does not have to be a traumatic experience. The lessons learned in both the Buddhist-and Christian-oriented courses at UVA changed my life.

My deepest gratitude extends to the College of William & Mary's Anthropology Department, which accepted me into their PhD program. Thanks are extended to my dissertation committee: Professors Tomoko Hamada Connolly, Danielle Moretti-Langholtz, Michael Blakey, and Jack Martin. A special note of thanks to Professor Emeritus Norman Barka, who did not appear to fear the controversy Powhatan oral tradition would induce. In addition, enormous support came from the College of William & Mary's vice president of student affairs, Sam Sadler, and his associates.

Unending personal support has come from my mom and dad, Edith and John Daniel; family members John, Joey, and Kitty; and friends Bob Haigh and Ruth and Bob Salzberg. Unexpected support, exceeding my wildest imagination, came from United Methodist Church members Stuart and Sylvia Woodcock. Last but certainly not least, my greatest supporter has been from Margie "Sunflower" Sargent, adopted daughter of the late Chief Daniel Webster "Little Eagle" Custalow. Many know of her ability to make dreams come true.

A special thank-you to the late Native scholar Vine Deloria Jr. and his protégé Steve Pavlik. Lin "Little Bear" and I were searching for Deloria to ask him to endorse *The True Story of Pocahontas*. Our hearts sank at learning of his passing. Within a few months, Pavlik contacted me. There is no question in our minds that Deloria was instrumental in causing this connection. As a result of our sense of a common bond, Pavlik eventually introduced *The True Story of Pocahontas* to Fulcrum Publishing.

Our deepest gratitude to Fulcrum Publishing for printing *The True Story of Pocahontas*, which had been silenced, especially in Virginia, for close to 400 years. Previous experience made me somewhat paranoid, wondering when the breaking off of a verbal agreement would occur. Fulcrum Publishing Associate Publisher and Vice President Sam Scinta must have sensed my uneasiness at such good news of Fulcrum's interest in the manuscript when he said, "We print Vine Deloria Jr.'s books; we are not afraid of anyone!" Much appreciation is also extended to Fulcrum

Publishing's managing editor, Katie Raymond. Raymond's comments and suggestions for change and/or further elaboration have truly improved this work. Thank you, dear friend Mary Anne Ruehling, for proofing the manuscript twice for us before and after the editor's suggestions.

It has been a great honor to work with Lin "Little Bear" on publishing the Mattaponi sacred oral history of Pocahontas. The honor bestowed upon me of carrying the sacred Powhatan history is one that I take very seriously. This history belongs to Pocahontas's people, the descendants of the Powhatan chiefdom. As a result, both Lin "Little Bear" and myself have agreed that all proceeds from the book will go into the Mattaponi Eagle Trust for Land Acquisition and Education for educational scholarships.

A special thank-you also goes out to Sheldon Franck for setting up this nonprofit trust and to his wife, Pam, and her mother, Louise Mabius, for their continual support.

This story of Pocahontas, part of the sacred Powhatan history, is larger than either Lin "Little Bear" or myself. It has been carried, protected, and maintained by the Mattaponi *quiak-ros* (priests) for nearly 400 years.

—Angela L. Daniel "Silver Star"

CHRONOLOGY OF EVENTS FROM 1580 TO 1618

A historical record compiled from both oral tradition and English documents.[1]

In 1580, John Smith was born in Willoughby, Lincolnshire, England.

In 1585, John Rolfe was born in Heacham, Norfolk, England. He was highly educated and from an old affluent Norfolk family.

In 1597/1598, Matoaka, better known as Pocahontas, was born to Chief Powhatan Wahunsenaca, commander in chief of the Powhatan nation, and his first wife, a Mattaponi named Pocahontas. Matoaka later chose her new name to be Pocahontas, after her mother, who died while giving birth to her. Her father often called her Pocahontas before she officially changed her name during her coming-of-age ceremony.

In December 1606, under the command of Captain Christopher Newport, three ships, the *Susan Constant, Godspeed,* and the *Discovery,* set sail from London to establish an English colony in the "New World."

In April 1607, Captain Christopher Newport and his ships sailed into Chesapeake Bay. The Jamestown fort was established a month later. The Powhatan welcomed the English. The Powhatan fed and helped the Jamestown settlers to survive the hardships they faced. Captain John Smith was twenty-seven years old. Pocahontas was a child of nine or ten years old.

In June 1607, Captain Christopher Newport sailed for England, leaving behind one ship, the *Discovery,* and 100 men. When he returned to the Virginia colony in January 1608, seven months later, he found that less than half the settlers he had left in June had survived.

In December 1607, Captain John Smith was captured by a Powhatan hunting party under the command of the Pamunkey Werowance Opechancanough, who took him to Chief Powhatan Wahunsenaca's village of Werowocomoco, the capital of the Powhatan nation, located on the north side of the Pamunkey (York) River.

In January 1608, Chief Powhatan Wahunseneca released Captain John Smith. Captain Christopher Newport returned from England the same day Smith returned to Jamestown.

In June 1608, Captain John Smith explored the territory of Chesapeake Bay and the Potomac River.

From September 1608 to September 1609, Captain John Smith was president of the Virginia colony.

In December 1608, Captain John Smith met with Chief Powhatan Wahunsenaca for the last time.

During the winter of 1608/1609, the Jamestown settlers were starving. Food and supplies had been depleted, and trading with the Powhatan was no longer possible as relationships were poor.

In the spring of 1609, John Rolfe and his English wife departed England for the "New World." They were shipwrecked in Bermuda. Their daughter, christened Bermuda, died in infancy while they were stranded.

In October 1609, Captain John Smith departed from Virginia, due to a gunpowder accident, never to return. The English colonists told Pocahontas that Smith died from the wounds.

In the spring of 1610, John Rolfe and his English wife arrived in Jamestown. The ship-wrecked crew had rebuilt two ships from the wreckage, now named the *Deliverance* and the *Patience*. It was Rolfe's intention to grow tobacco.

The winter of 1609/1610 is remembered by the English colonists as the "starving time." Only sixty of the original 500 colonists survived the winter the *Deliverance* and *Patience* arrived. With Captain John Smith gone, the colonists were afraid to ask the Powhatan for help.

Sometime afterward, Pocahontas came of age. She was about thirteen years old. Pocahontas fell in love with and married Kocoum, an elite Potowomac warrior and guard at Werowo-comoco. They eventually moved to the Potowomac tribe and had a child. According to William Deyo, Tribal Historian of the Patawomeck Tribe and descendant of Pocahontas and Kocoum, their offspring was a girl, named Ka-Okee (email communication, n.owl@att.net, November 4, 2021).

In 1612, only two years after he arrived in Jamestown, John Rolfe's first crop of West Indies tobacco was curing. It was taller than the Powhatan type of tobacco.

In 1612, Captain Samuel Argall, a navigator and trader, arrived in the New World.

In April 1613, Pocahontas was kidnapped from the village of the Potowomac on the Potomac River and taken to Jamestown, where she was held prisoner. Pocahontas was moved from Jamestown to Henrico within three months.

Later in 1613, John Rolfe received word that his tobacco was getting close to being comparable to others on the market. But it was lacking in quality and fell short of bringing competitive prices. Rolfe started helping Reverend Alexander Whitaker teach Christianity to Pocahontas.

In March 1614, almost a year after Pocahontas was abducted, she was taken by Sir Thomas Dale, along with about 150 men and John Rolfe, to one of Chief Powhatan Wahunsenaca's villages to settle her ransom. Volleys of arrows ensued. Pocahontas was permitted to speak to two of her brothers. The English leaders spoke with Pamunkey Werowance Opechan-canough, who requested more time to pay the balance of the ransom, to wait until the harvest of crops.[2]

Soon afterward, Pocahontas was baptized. She was given the Christian name Rebecca. It is believed that Sir Thomas Dale and Reverend Alexander Whitaker were present at the baptism. John Rolfe asked Dale for permission to marry Pocahontas. Dale consented. Dale was the governor of the Virginia colony for three months during the summer of 1611 and deputy governor from March 1614 to April 1616.

In April 1614, Pocahontas and John Rolfe were married in a church at Jamestown. It was a second marriage for both Pocahontas and Rolfe. He was twenty-nine years old. Pocahontas was sixteen or seventeen years old.

Later in 1614, John Rolfe was counseled by the Powhatan *quiakros* (priests) as to the best methods for growing and curing tobacco in Virginia. Rolfe focused his attention on tobacco farming. Rolfe received an extensive piece of land in Henrico from Sir Thomas Dale. With the help of the Powhatan *quiakros*, Rolfe began to produce fine tobacco.

1616 was the designated deadline by the Virginia Company of London for returns to be evident to the investors in the Virginia colony.

In the spring of 1616, Captain Samuel Argall sets sail for London on the *Treasurer*. The Virginia Company arranged the trip. Aboard were Pocahontas, John Rolfe, their son, Thomas, and a cargo of tobacco grown by Rolfe for trial in England. Also aboard were Sir Thomas Dale and nearly a dozen Powhatan, including Uttamattamakin, a Powhatan priest, and his wife, Mattachanna, who was Pocahontas's oldest sister.

In March 1617, Pocahontas, John Rolfe, and Thomas began a return trip to Virginia, again with Captain Samuel Argall at the helm. Pocahontas suddenly died on ship, and the ship returned to Gravesend, England, where she is buried.

In May 1617, Captain Samuel Argall became governor of the Virginia colony. He remained governor until April 1619.

In 1617, exports of Virginia tobacco to England and Bermuda totaled 20,000 pounds.

In the spring of 1618, Chief Powhatan Wahunsenaca died from grief, nearly a year after Pocahontas's death.

In June 1618, the *George* carried 20,000 pounds of Virginia-grown tobacco to England. Total exports doubled.

ENDNOTES

Introduction: How To Tell the Story?

1. John Smith, "The Generall Historie, The Second Book," [1624] in *The Complete Works of Captain John Smith (1580–1631) Vol. II*, ed. Philip L. Barbour (Chapel Hill: The University of North Carolina Press, 1986), 126. Smith and Dr. Linwood "Little Bear" Custalow are in agreement: "[A]s the Country call Powhatan, Arrohateck, Appamatuck, Pamaunkee, Youghtanund, and Mattapanient." Helen C. Rountree, *Pocahontas's People: The Powhatan Indians of Virginia through Four Centuries* (Norman and London: University of Oklahoma Press, 1990), 10. Rountree advocates that Chiskiack was one of the six core Powhatan tribes, instead of Youghtanund. "Powhatan claimed to rule nearly all of eastern Virginia. He had inherited six chiefdoms (Powhatan, Arrohateck, Appamuattuck, Pamunkey, Mattaponi, and Chiskiack) and had then gathered more tribes into his fold, either by warfare or by intimidation."

2. Christain F. Feest, *The Powhatan Tribes*, ed. Frank W. Porter III (New York: Chelsea House, 1989), 14.

Chapter One: Pocahontas: A Favorite Child

1. William Strachey, *The Historie of Travaile into Virginia Britinia (1612)* (London: The Hakluyt Society, 1849), 47–48. Strachey states that Powhatan is

> called by sondry names, according to his divers places, qualityes or honours by himself obteyned, either for his valour his government, or some such like goodness, which they vse to admire and commend to succeeding tymes, with memorable Tytles, and so Commonly they of greatest merritt amongst them aspire to many names.
>
> That great Emperour at this tyme amongst them we Commonly call Powhatan for by that name yt is, he was made known vnto vs, when we aryved in the Country first, and so indeed he was generall called when he as was a young man, as taking his denomynacion from the Country Powhatan, wherein he was born, which is at the falls as before mencioned ... the Inhabitants themselues especially his frontier neighbour princes, call him still Powhatan, his owne people sometymes call him Ottaniack, sometymes Mananatowick, which last signifyes great Kinge, but his proper right name which they salute him with (himself in presence) is Wahunsenacawh.

2. ———, *The Historie of Travaile into Virginia Britinia (1612)*, 111.

3. Helen C. Rountree, *Young Pocahontas in the Indian World* (Yorktown, VA: J & R Graphic Services, 1995), 2. Rountree states that Pocahontas's mother's name and tribal affiliation are unknown because it was not recorded in the English writings. Rountree assumed Pocahontas's mother survived childbirth.

4. Samuel Purchase, "An Interview in London" in *Jamestown Narratives: Eyewitness Accounts of the Virginia Colony, the First Decade: 1607–1617*, ed. Edward Wright Haile (Champlain, VA: RoundHouse, 2001), 882.

5. Strachey, *The Historie of Travaile into Virginia Britinia*, 56. "Parahunt, one of Powhatan's sonnes, whome we therefore call Tanxpowatan, which is much to say Little Powhatan, and is weroance of the country which hath his own name, called Powhatan, lying (as

before mencioned) close under the Falls, bordering the Monacans, and he maye at the present be furnished fifty fighting and ready men."

6. Ibid., 60: "Pochins, one of Powhatan's sonns at Kecoughtan, and was the young weroance there at the same tyme when Sir Thomas Gates, liuetenant-general, took possession of yt."

Chapter Two: Captain John Smith: An English Chief

1. John Smith, "A True Relation" in *Jamestown Narratives: Eyewitness Accounts of the Virginia Colony, the First Decade: 1607–1617*, ed. Edward Wright Haile (Champlain, VA: RoundHouse, 2001), 181.

2. Helen C. Rountree, *The Powhatan Indians of Virginia: Their Traditional Culture* (Norman: University of Oklahoma Press, 1989), 13. Tsenacomoco was the name of the Powhatan sociopolitical entity. In *The Historie of Travaile into Virginia Britinia* (London: The Hakluyt Society, 1849), William Strachey recorded, "The severall territoryes and provinces which are in chief commaunded by their great king Powhatan, are Comprehended vnder the denomynation of Tsenacommacoh ... " (37) and "Which wee call Virginia Britania, by the Inhabitans as aforesaid *Tsenacommacoh*, is governed in chief by a great king ... " (56).

3. Smith, "The Generall Historie of Virginia" in *The Complete Works of Captain John Smith (1580–1631)*, ed. Philip L. Barbour (Chapel Hill: University of North Carolina Press, 1986), 126. Smith and Dr. Linwood "Little Bear" Custalow are in agreement: "[A] s the Country call Powhatan, Arrohateck, Appamatuck, Pamaunkee, Youghtanund, and Mattapanient." In *Pocahontas's People: The Powhatan Indians of Virginia through Four Centuries* (Norman: University of Oklahoma, 1990), Rountree advocated that Chiskiack was one of the six core Powhatan tribes, instead of Youghtanund. "Powhatan claimed to rule nearly all of eastern Virginia. He had inherited six chiefdoms (Powhatan, Arrohateck, Appamuattuck, Pamunkey, Mattaponi, and Chiskiack) and had then gathered more tribes into his fold, either by warfare or by intimidation" (10).

4. William Strachey, *The Historie of Travaile into Virginia Britinia (1612)* (London: The Hakluyt Society, 1849), 100. "When they [the Powhatan Indians] intend any warrs, the weroances usually advise with their priests or conjurers, their allies and best trusted chouncellors and friends; but commonly the priest have the resulting voice, and determyne therefore their resolutions."

5. George Percy, *Observations Gathered out of "A Discourse of the Plantation of the Southern Colony in Virginia by the English, 1606,"* ed. David B. Quinn (Charlottesville: University Press of Virginia, 1967), 12–13, 25–27. According to the English account by George Percy, who arrived with the first party in 1607, the Powhatan Indians constantly extended hospitalities of welcome and food to the English upon their arrival.

6. Smith, "A True Relation" and "The Generall Historie of Virginia" in *The Complete Works of Captain John Smith (1580–1631)*, ed. Philip L. Barbour (Chapel Hill: University of North Carolina Press, 1986). In "A True Relation," a letter to a friend, Smith estimated that 200 Powhatan bowmen captured him; whereas in his later publication, "The Generall Historie of Virginia," Smith wrote that it was 300 Powhatan bowmen (47; 146–147).

7. ———, "A True Relation" in *Jamestown Narratives*, 179. The English account of Captain John Smith's capture includes the "Paspaheh, the Chickahamanian (Chickahominy), Youghtanum (Youghtanund), Pamaunka (Pamunkey), Mattapanient (Mattaponi), and Kiskiack."

8. Ibid., 161.

9. Alvin M. Josephy Jr., *500 Nations* (New York: Knopf, 1994), 144.

10. For more detailed information about the effects of Hernando de Soto's campaign in the southeastern present-day United States, see pages 140–153 of *500 Nations*.

11. For information on the Spanish rendition of the story Don Luis, see *The Spanish Jesuit Mission in Virginia 1570–1572* by Clifford M. Lewis and Albert J. Loomie (Chapel Hill: Published for the Virginia Historical Society by the University of North Carolina, 1953).

12. Lewis and Loomie, *The Spanish Jesuit Mission in Virginia 1570–1572*, 51–55.

13. Conway Whittle Sams, *The Conquest of Virginia: The Third Attempt 1610–1624* (New York: G. P. Putnam's Sons, 1939), 343, and Alexander Brown, *The First Republic in America: An Account of the Origin of This Nation, Written from the Records Then (1624) Concealed by the Council, Rather Than from the Histories Then Licensed by the Crown* (New York: Russell & Russell, 1969), 210.

14. Charles E. Hatch Jr., *The First Seventeen Years—Virginia, 1607–1624* (Charlottesville: University Press of Virginia, 1957), 3.

15. Smith, "A True Relation" in *Jamestown Narratives*, 167. Smith wrote, "This so contented him [Chief Powhatan] as immediately, with [our] attentive silence, with a loud oration he proclaimed me a werowanes of Powhaton and that all his subjects should so esteem us, and no man account us strangers nor Paspaheghans, but Powhatans, and that the corn, women, and country should be to us as to his own people, but with the best languages and signs of thanks I could express, I took my leave."

16. Ibid., 165. "The Emperor Powhatan each week one or twice sent me many presents of deer, bread, *raugroughcuns* [raccoons], half always for my father [Captain Newport], whom he desired to see, and half for me, and so continually importuned by messengers and presents that I would come to fetch the corn and take the country their king [Chief Powhatan] had given me [Capahowasick], as at last Captain Newport resolved to see him."

17. Ibid., 161. "He [Chief Powhatan] kindly welcomed me with good words and great platters of sundry victuals, assuring me his friendship and my liberty within four days."

18. Ibid., Smith established early on with Chief Powhatan that the English and the Spaniards were enemies. After Chief Powhatan assured Smith he would be released in four days, "He [Chief Powhatan] asked me the cause of our coming. I told him, being in fight with the Spaniards our enemy, being overpow'red, near put to retreat, and by extreme weather put to this shore. … "

19. Ibid., 164–165.

Chapter Three: Pocahontas: The Powhatan Peace Symbol

1. William Strachey, *The Historie of Travaile into Virginia Britinia (1612)* (London: The Hakluyt Society, 1849), 65. "[A]nd therefore would the before remembered Pochahuntas, a well featured, but wanton yong girle, Powhatan's daughter, sometymes resorting to our fort, of the age then of eleven or twelve yeares, get the boyes forth with her into the market place, and make them wheele, falling on their hand, turning up their heeles upwards, whome she would followe and wheele so her self, naked as she was, all the fort over. … "

2. John Smith, "A True Relation" in *Jamestown Narratives: Eyewitness Accounts of the Virginia Colony, the First Decade: 1607–1617*, ed. Edward Wright Haile (Champlain, VA: RoundHouse, 2001), 181. "This he [Powhatan] sent his most trusty messenger, called Rawhunt, as much exceeding in deformity of person, but of a subtle wit and

crafty understanding. He with a long circumstance told me how well Powhatan loved and respected me and, in that I should not doubt any way his kindness, he had sent his child [Pocahontas], which he most esteemed, to see me, [and] a deer and bread besides for a present. ... "

3. Paula Gunn Allen, *Pocahontas: Medicine Woman, Spy, Entrepreneur, Diplomat* (San Francisco: Harper, 2003).

Chapter Four: Powhatan Moral: Not by Force

1. John Smith, "The General History" in *Jamestown Narratives: Eyewitness Accounts of the Virginia Colony, The First Decade: 1607–1617*, ed. Edward Wright Haile (Champlain, VA: RoundHouse, 2001), 311. Smith wrote: "We searched also the countries of Youghtanund and Mattapanient, where the people imparted that little they had with such complaints and tears from the eyes of women and children as he [Smith is writing in the third person] had been too cruel to have been a Christian that would not have been satisfied and moved with compassion."

2. Ibid., 197, 301. Smith quotes Chief Powhatan,

> Captain Smith, I never use any werowance so kindly as yourself, yet from you I receive the least kindness of any. Captain Newport gave me swards, copper, clothes, a bed, tools, or what I desired, ever taking what I offered him; and would send away his guns when I entreated him. None doth deny to lie at my feet or refuse to do what I desire, but only you; of whom I can have nothing but what you regard not, and yet you will have whatsoever you demand. Captain Newport you call father, and so you call me. But I see for all us both you will do what you list, wand we must both seek to content you. But if you intend so friendly as you say, send hence your arms that I may believe you. For you see the love I bear you doth cause me thus nakedly to forget myself.

In the last sentence, Chief Powhatan is asking Smith why he will not disarm himself, as he, Chief Powhatan, has done in Smith's presence.

3. Smith, "The Generall Historie of Virginia" in *The Complete Works of Captain John Smith (1580–1631)*, ed. Philip L. Barbour (Chapel Hill: University of North Carolina Press, 1986), 196, and "The General History" in *Jamestown Narratives*, 299.

4. ———, "The General History" in *Jamestown Narratives*, 303. Smith writes: "For Pocahontas, his dearest jewel and daughter, in that dark night came through the irksome woods and told our captain great cheer should be sent us by and by. But, Powhatan and all the power he could make would after come kill us all if they that brought it could not kill us with our own weapons when we were at supper. Therefore if we would live she wished us presently to be gone. Such things as she delighted in he would have given her, but with the tears running down her cheeks she said she durst not be seen to have any, for if Powhatan should know it, she were but dead, and so she ran away by herself as she came."

5. Ibid.

6. Ibid., 304.

7. Ibid., 307.

8. Ibid.

9. Helen C. Rountree, *Pocahontas's People: The Powhatan Indians of Virginia through Four*

Centuries (Norman: University of Oklahoma Press, 1990), 74–75. For Smith's writings on the topic, see *The Complete Works of Captain John Smith (1580–1631)*, 293–294.

Chapter Five: Danger in Pocahontas's Homeland

1. William Waller Hening, *The Statutes at Large; Being a Collection of All the Laws of Virginia, from the First Session of the Legislature, in the Year 1619, Vol. I* (New York: R. & W. & G. Bartow, 1823), 410. The March 31, 1655, Act II states that Indians are not to be killed within English territory unless doing something mischievous. No Indians to be entertained without license from the county court or two justices of the peace. Indian children can be servants, by leave of their parents, if the children are educated and brought up in the Christian religion.

2. ————, *The Statutes at Large; Being a Collection of All the Laws of Virginia, from the First Session of the Legislature, in the Year 1619, Vol. III* (Philadelphia: Thomas Desilver, 1823), 298. The October 1705 XXXI entry states that Indians, Negroes, mulattos, and non-Christians are not allowed to be witnesses in cases of law.

3. Charles E. Hatch Jr., *The First Seventeen Years—Virginia, 1607–1624* (Charlottesville: University Press of Virginia, 1957) and Conway Whittle Sams, *The Conquest of Virginia: The Third Attempt 1610–1624* (New York: G. P. Putnam's Sons, 1939).

4. Ibid.

5. John Smith, "The General History" in *Jamestown Narratives: Eyewitness Accounts of the Virginia Colony, The First Decade: 1607–1617*, ed. Edward Wright Haile (Champlain, VA: RoundHouse, 2001), 864. Smith recorded Pocahontas's response to him while in London: "They [colonists in her homeland] did tell us always you were dead, and I knew no other till I came to Plymouth. Yet Powhatan did command Uttamatomakkin to seek you, and know the truth, because your countrymen will lie much."

6. Mattaponi oral history did not have an account of Smith's leaving. According to "The General History" in *Jamestown Narratives*, he was involved with a gunpowder accident (332). "Sleeping in his boat—for the ship was returned two days before—accidentally [some]one fired his powder bag, which tore the flesh from his body and thighs nine or ten inches square in a most pitiful manner." After the accident, Smith returned to England (334).

7. Ibid., 332.

Chapter Six: Pocahontas Comes of Age

1. William Strachey, *The Historie of Travaile into Virginia Britinia (1612)* (London: The Hakluyt Society, 1849), 94, and John Smith, "The Generall Historie of Virginia" in *The Complete Works of Captain John Smith (1580–1631)*, ed. Philip L. Barbour (Chapel Hill: University of North Carolina Press, 1986), 124.

2. Strachey, *The Historie of Travaile into Virginia Britinia*, 54: "Younge Pocohunta, a daughter of his [Chief Powhatan], using sometyme to our fort [Jamestown] in tymes past, nowe married to a private captaine, called Kocoum, some two years since."

Chapter Seven: Pocahontas Kidnapped

1. Pocahontas's closest relatives were her father, Chief Powhatan Wahunsenaca; Chief Powhatan's counselor priest, Uttamattakin, and his wife, Mattachanna, Wahunsenaca's eldest daughter; and Pocahontas's husband, Kocoum.

2. Samuel Argall's account of the capture of Pocahontas in a letter from 1613 in *Pocahontas and Her Companions: A Chapter from the History of the Virginia Company of London*,

ed. Reverend Edward D. Neill (Albany, NY: Joel Munsell, 1869), 7: "I was told by certaine Indians y friends that the great Powhatan's daughter Pokahunits was with the great King Patawomek whether I presently repaired resolving to possesse myselfe of her by any stratagem that I could use for the ransoming of so many Englishmen as were prisoners with Powhatan as also to get such armes and tooles as hee and other Indians had got by murther and stealing some others of our nation, with some quantity of corne for the colonies reliefe."

3. Wesley Frank Craven, *The Virginia Company of London, 1606–1624* (Williamsburg: Virginia 350th Anniversary Celebration Corporation, 1957), 31.

4. Samuel Argall's account of the capture of Pocahontas in a letter from 1613 in *Pocahontas and Her Companions*, 7.

5. Ibid., 7–8: "[H]e repaired presently to his brother the great King of Patawomeck, who being made acquainted with the matter called his counsell together and after some few houres deliberation concluded rather to deliver her into my boat, when I carried her aboard my ship."

6. Ibid. Argall reported Japazaw's response: "He alleaged that if hee undertake the businesse, then Powhatan would make warres upon him and his people. ... "

7. Ibid. Argall's answer to Japazaws: "[B]ut upon my promise that I would joyne with him against him [Powhatan]. ... "

8. Ibid., 755: " ... I could use [Pocahontas] for the ransoming of so many Englishmen as were prisoners with Powhatan, as also to get such arms and tools as he and other Indians had got by murther [murder] abd stealing from others of our nation, with some quantity of corn for the colony's relief."

9. Ibid.

10. Frederic W. Gleach, *Powhatan's World and Colonial Virginia: A Conflict of Cultures* (Lincoln: University of Nebraska Press, 1997), 56–58.

11. *The New World*, written and directed by Terrence Malick, 2005, filmstrip.

12. Jeffrey L. Hantman, "Between Powhatan and Quirank: Reconstructing Monacan Culture and History in the Context of Jamestown" in *American Anthropologist* 92, no. 3 (September 1990): 676–690.

13. John Smith, "The Generall Historie of Virginia" in *The Complete Works of Captain John Smith (1580–1631)*, ed. Philip L. Barbour (Chapel Hill: University of North Carolina Press, 1986), 243.

14. Deyo, William, Tribal Historian of the Patawomeck Tribe and descendant of Pocahontas and Kocoum and their daughter, Ka-Okee. Email communication via n.owl@att.net, November 4, 2021.

15. John Smith, "the Generall Historie of Virginia" in *The Complete Works of Captain John Smith (1580–1631)*, 243.

Chapter Eight: No Retaliation

1. Angela L. Daniel, "The Spirituality of Virginia Powhatan Indians and Their Descendents: Living Spirituality," unpublished religious studies master's thesis (Charlottesville: University of Virginia, May 2003).

2. Roy Harvey Pearce, *The Savages of America: A Study of the Indian and the Idea of Civilization* (Baltimore: Johns Hopkins Press, 1965), 3–5. Pearce clearly stated that the English considered the Indians to be savages. According to Pearce, the English perceived the Indians with such inferiority that they became the standard of what not be. The English arrived with the preconception that the Natives were neither civilized nor Christian; consequently "they did not fully partake of the divine idea of order."

3. Carl Bridenbaugh, *Jamestown 1544–1699* (New York: Oxford University Press, 1980), 62–63. Bridenbaugh makes it clear that three leaders within the Virginia colony, Alexander Whitaker, Sir Thomas Dale, and John Rolfe, were close associates. They were bonded by their Calvinistic beliefs and similar aspirations for the colony. They all lived in close proximity to each other in the Virginia colony. John Rolfe arrived in Jamestown in June 1610 and experimented with varieties of tobacco crops (Louise Heath Foley, *Henrico Parish and Its Early Parishioners* [Richmond: Virginia Historial Society, 1981]). Both Alexander Whitaker and Sir Thomas Dale left England together and arrived in the Virginia colony in 1611 (Samuel S. Hill, *Encyclopedia of Religion in the South*, 1984, 840; Charles E. Hatch Jr., *The First Seventeen Years—Virginia, 1607–1624*, 12). Devout Calvinists, Whitaker, Dale, and Rolfe worked in consort in strengthening the colony via Calvinistic influences, fulfilling Virginia Company's threefold religious, political, and economic goals. Whitaker promoted Calvinism in the Virginia colony by serving two settlement churches, in Henrico and Bemuda Hundreds (Hill 1984, 841). Sir Thomas Dale enforced Calvinism by promoting a political structure and by serving as deputy governor of Virginia (Hatch 1957, 12). Dale is famous for the enforcement of the "Lawes Divine, Moral and Martial." Bridenbaugh stated, "Foremost among the Puritan rules was Governor Dale, whose Sabbath laws would have won approval from strictest English Puritans." Scholar Sanford H. Cobb in *The Rise of Religious Liberty in America: A History* (New York: Burt Franklin, 1902) agreed with Bridenbaugh, stating that these laws "were of severity far exceeding any of the more famous Puritan restrictions in New England" (77).

4. John Smith, "The Generall Historie of Virginia" in *The Complete Works of Captain John Smith (1580–1631)*, ed. Philip L. Barbour (Chapel Hill: University of North Carolina Press, 1986), 251.

5. Ralph Hamor, "A True Discourse of the Present Estate of Virginia" in *Jamestown Narratives: Eyewitness Accounts of the Virginia Colony, the First Decade: 1607–1617*, ed. Edward Wright Haile (Champlain, VA: RoundHouse, 2001), 806.

6. William M. S. Rasmussen and Robert S. Tilton, *Pocahontas: Her Life and Legend* (Richmond: Virginia Historical Society, 1994), 23.

7. Smith, "The Generall Historie of Virginia" in *The Complete Works of Captain John Smith (1580–1631)*, 258.

8. Rasmussen and Tilton, *Pocahontas: Her Life and Legend*, 23.

9. Ibid.

10. Smith, "The Generall Historie of Virginia" in *The Complete Works of Captain John Smith (1580–1631)*, 251: "[A]fter she had beene some time thus tutored, shee never had desire to goe to her father [Chief Powhatan Wahunsenaca], nor could well endure the society of her owne nation … she openly renounced her countries idolatry, confessed the faith of Christ, and was baptized."

Chapter Nine: Marriage in Captivity

1. Mattaponi oral tradition states that Mattachanna's birth name was Channa. At her coming-of-age ceremony, her *huskanasquaw*, Channa added *Matta* to her name. *Matta* was to distinguish her as being the daughter of her father's Mattaponi wife, the wife he chose as his beloved and not one given to him out of alliance. Uttamattamakin was a priest of the highest order, as the *Utta* in his name signifies. *Matta* signifies his tribe, the Mattaponi. *Makin* was his name otherwise. *Utta* is the prefix for the Uttamussac Temple, also known as the Powhatan temple, which was the resting place for the Powhatan chiefs, as well as their place of worship. These were the two individuals

who stayed with and cared for Pocahontas.

2. Chief George "Thunder Cloud" F. Custalow was Dr. Lin "Little Bear's" grandfather. Chief George, along with Chief O. T. Custalow, Dr. Lin "Little Bear's" uncle, and Chief Daniel Webster "Little Eagle" Custalow, Dr. Lin "Little Bear's" father, were the primary elders in his life who taught him the sacred oral history maintained in the Mattaponi tribe.

3. These are classic signs of first-trimester pregnancy.

4. David C. Steinmetz, *Calvin in Context* (New York: Oxford University Press, 1995), 5. Reverend Alexander Whitaker was known as the "Apostle of Virginia."

5. William M. S. Rasmussen and Robert S. Tilton, *Pocahontas: Her Life and Legend* (Richmond: Virginia Historical Society, 1994), 23.

6. Helen C. Rountree, *Pocahontas's People: The Powhatan Indians of Virginia through Four Centuries* (Norman: University of Oklahoma Press, 1990), 299: "The actual date of Thomas Rolfe's birth was not recorded." The birth of Thomas, acknowledged as the son of Pocahontas and John Rolfe, is often given by scholars as occurring in 1615, if a date is noted at all. Based on Smith's "The Generall Historie of Virginia," it is generally assumed that Thomas was born after Pocahontas submitted to marrying John Rolfe in a Christian ceremony in April 1614 (245–246).

7. John Rolfe to Sir Thomas Dale, Virginia, 1614, in *Jamestown Narratives: Eyewitness Accounts of the Virginia Colony, The First Decade: 1607–1617*, ed. Edward Wright Haile (Champlain, VA: RoundHouse, 2001), 851. Handwritten copy made by Conway Robinson from a Dutch copy of the original in the Bodleian Library in Oxford, England. Photocopy made at The Virginia Historical Society, Richmond, Virginia, 2002.

8. John Smith, "The General History" in *Jamestown Narratives*, 336. Smith wrote, "Some prophetical spirit calculated he had the savages in such subjection he would have made himself a king by marrying Pocahontas, Powhatan's daughter."

9. Ibid. "But her marriage could no way have entitled him by any right to the kingdom, nor was it ever suspected he had ever such a thought, or more regarded her, or any of them, than in honest reason and discretion he might."

10. Ibid. "It is true she was the very nonpareil of his kingdom, and at most not past 13 or 14 of age."

11. Ralph Hamor, "A True Discourse of the Present Estate of Virginia" in *Jamestown Narratives*, 833–834.

Chapter Ten: The Colony Saved by the Powhatan

1. W. Stitt Robinson Jr., *Mother Earth: Land Grants in Virginia, 1607–1699* (Baltimore: Clearfield, 1957), 14–15. Robinson noted, "Both adventurer and planter were promised a proportionate share of any dividends distributed, whether in land or in money. The joint-stock arrangement was originally set to continue seven years from its inception in 1609, thus making 1616 as the terminal date. During this period monetary dividends might be declared, and at the end of the period the land suitable for cultivation was to be divided with at least 100 acres to be given for each share of stock."

2. W. M. Clark, ed., *Colonial Churches in the Original Colony of Virginia, Second Edition* (Richmond: Southern Churchman Company, 1908).

3. John Smith, "A True Relation" in *Jamestown Narratives: Eyewitness Accounts of the Virginia Colony, the First Decade: 1607–1617*, ed. Edward Wright Haile (Champlain, VA: RoundHouse, 2001), 161.

4. Julian Alvin Carroll Chandler and T. B. Thames, *Colonial Virginia* (Richmond: Times-Dispatch, 1907), 35.

5. Ibid.

6. Ibid., 40.

7. The Jamestown Foundation, *Story of John Rolfe, Who Saved a Colony and Planted the Seeds of a Nation* (Published to commemorate the 350th anniversary of John Rolfe's first harvest, 1957), 6.

8. Ibid., 9.

9. Ibid., 6.

10. Ibid., 7. *The Story of John Rolfe* states that it is likely that Pocahontas provided Powhatan knowledge of tobacco management to Rolfe.

11. Ibid., 11.

12. Helen C. Rountree, *Pocahontas's People: The Powhatan Indians of Virginia through Four Centuries* (Norman: University of Oklahoma Press, 1990), 299: Roundtree states in endnote number 67 that Thomas Rolfe was born prior to the voyage to England in 1616. However, the actual date of Thomas Rolfe's birth was not recorded.

13. Ibid., 62.

14. John Smith, "The Generall Historie of Virginia" in *The Complete Works of Captain John Smith (1580–1631)*, ed. Philip L. Barbour (Chapel Hill: University of North Carolina Press, 1986), 261.

15. William Strachey, *The Historie of Travaile into Virginia Britinia (1612)* (London: The Hakluyt Society, 1849), 100: "When they [the Powhatan Indians] intend any warrs, the weroances usually advise with their priests or conjurers, their allies and best trusted chouncellors and friends; but commonly the priest have the resulting voice, and determyne therefore their resolutions."

16. Uttamatomakkin (Tomocomo), "An Interview in London" in *Jamestown Narratives: Eyewitness Accounts of the Virginia Colony, the First Decade: 1607–1617*, ed. Edward Wright Haile (Champlain, VA: RoundHouse, 2001), 880–883.

17. The Jamestown Foundation, *The Story of John Rolfe, Who Saved a Colony and Planted the Seeds of a Nation*, 9.

18. William Waller Hening, *The Statutes at Large; Being a Collection of All the Laws of Virginia from the First Session of the Legislature in the Year 1619, Vol. 1* (New York: R. & W. & G. Bartow, 1823).

19. Smith, "A True Relation" in *Jamestown Narratives*, 871–872.

Chapter Eleven: Pocahontas's Revelation

1. John Smith, "The Generall Historie of Virginia" in *The Complete Works of Captain John Smith (1580–1631)*, ed. Philip L. Barbour (Chapel Hill: University of North Carolina Press, 1986), 260–261.

Chapter Twelve: Murder in England

1. John Smith, "The Generall Historie of Virginia" in *The Complete Works of Captain John Smith (1580–1631)*, ed. Philip L. Barbour (Chapel Hill: University of North Carolina Press, 1986), 262.

2. Carl Bridenbaugh, *Jamestown 1544–1699* (New York: Oxford University Press, 1980).

3. Smith, "A True Relation" in *The Complete Works of Captain John Smith (1580–1631)*, 173.

4. Helen C. Rountree, *Pocahontas's People: The Powhatan Indians of Virginia through Four Centuries* (Norman: University of Oklahoma Press, 1990), 10: "Powhatan's successor

was therefore his next brother, Opitchapam, a lame and unimpressive man who was overshadowed in his lifetime by his more able and charismatic brother and successor, Opechancanough."

Epilogue: In the Years That Followed

1. William Waller Hening, *The Statutes at Large; Being a Collection of All the Laws of Virginia, from the First Session of the Legislature, in the Year 1619, Vol. I* (New York: R. & W. & G. Bartow, 1823), 153.

2. Martha W. McCartney, *Documentary History of Jamestown Island, Vol. 1: Narrative History.* Jamestown Archaeological Assessment 1992–1996 series. (Williamsburg, VA: Colonial Williamsburg Foundation, 2000), 327.

3. Helen C. Rountree, *Pocahontas's People: The Powhatan Indians of Virginia through Four Centuries* (Norman: University of Oklahoma Press, 1990), 62.

4. W. Stitt Robinson Jr., *Mother Earth: Land Grants in Virginia, 1607–1699* (Baltimore: Clearfield, 1957), 16.

5. Susan Myra Kingsbury, ed., *The Records of the Virginia Company of London, Vol. I* (Washington: Government Printing Office, 1906–1935), 224.

6. McCartney, *Documentary History of Jamestown Island, Vol. III: Biographies of Owners and Residents.* Jamestown Archaeological Assessment 1992–1996 series. (Williamsburg, VA: Colonial Williamsburg Foundation, 2000), 17.

7. McCartney, *Documentary History of Jamestown Island, Vol. 1: Narrative History*, 307.

8. Kingsbury, *The Records of the Virginia Company of London, Vol. IV* (Washington: Government Printing Office, 1906–1935), 551, 555–556.

9. McCartney, *Documentary History of Jamestown Island, Vol. 1: Narrative History*, 305.

10. Edward Wright Haile, ed., *Jamestown Narratives: Eyewitness Accounts of the Virginia Colony, The First Decade: 1607–1617* (Champlain, Virginia: RoundHouse, 2001), 55.

11. The Jamestown Foundation, *The Story of John Rolfe, Who Saved a Colony and Planted the Seeds of a Nation.* (Published to commemorate the 350th anniversary of John Rolfe's first harvest, 1957), 6.

12. Ibid.

13. Ibid.

14. John Smith, "The Generall Historie of Virginia," in *The Complete Works of Captain John Smith (1580–1631)*, ed. Philip L. Barbour (Chapel Hill: University of North Carolina Press, 1986), 245–246.

15. Jamestown Foundation, *The Story of John Rolfe*, 7. It is likely that Pocahontas provided Powhatan knowledge of tobacco management to Rolfe.

16. Ibid., 11.

17. Ibid., 10–11.

Chronology

1. William W. Abbot, *A Virginia Chronology 1585–1783* (Charlottesville: University of Virginia Press, 1970) for the English-based chronology.

2. John Smith, "The Generall Historie of Virginia," in *The Complete Works of Captain John Smith (1580–1631)*, ed. Philip L. Barbour (Chapel Hill: University of North Carolina Press, 1986), 244–245.

BIBLIOGRAPHY

Abbot, William W. *A Virginia Chronology 1585–1783*. Charlottesville: University of Virginia Press, 1970.

Allen, Paula Gunn. *Pocahontas: Medicine Woman, Spy, Entrepreneur, Diplomat*. San Francisco: Harper, 2003.

Argall, Samuel. Letter from 1613 in *Pocahontas and Her Companions: A Chapter from the History of the Virginia Company of London*. Ed. Reverend Edward D. Neill. Albany, NY: Joel Munsell, 1869.

Bridenbaugh, Carl. *Jamestown 1544–1699*. New York: Oxford University Press, 1980.

Brown, Alexander. *The First Republic in America: An Account of the Origin of This Nation, Written from the Records Then (1624) Concealed by the Council, Rather Than from the Histories Then Licensed by the Crown*. New York: Russell & Russell, 1969.

Chandler, Julian Alvin Carroll, and T. B. Thames. *Colonial Virginia*. Richmond: Times-Dispatch, 1907.

Clark, W. M., ed. *Colonial Churches in the Original Colony of Virginia, Second Edition*. Richmond: Southern Churchman Company, 1908.

Cobb, Sanford H. *The Rise of Religious Liberty in America: A History*. New York: Burt Franklin, 1902.

Craven, Wesley Frank. *The Virginia Company of London, 1606–1624*. Williamsburg: Virginia 350th Anniversary Celebration Corporation, 1957.

Daniel, Angela L. "The Spirituality of Virginia Powhatan Indians and Their Descendents: Living Spirituality." Unpublished religious studies master's thesis. Charlottesville: University of Virginia, May 2003.

Deyo, William. Tribal Historian of the Patawomeck Tribe and descendant of Pocahontas and Kocoum and their daughter, Ka-Okee. Email communication via n.owl@att.net, November 4, 2021.

Feest, Christain F. *The Powhatan Tribes*. Ed. Frank W. Porter III. New York: Chelsea House, 1989.

Foley, Louise Heath. *Henrico Parish and Its Early Parishioners*. Richmond: Virginia Historical Society, 1981.

Gleach, Frederic W. *Powhatan's World and Colonial Virginia, A Conflict of Cultures*. Lincoln: University of Nebraska Press. 1997.

Haile, Edward Wright, ed. *Jamestown Narratives: Eyewitness Accounts of the Virginia Colony, The First Decade: 1607–1617*. Champlain, VA: RoundHouse, 2001.

Hamor, Ralph. "A True Discourse of the Present Estate of Virginia" in *Jamestown Narratives: Eyewitness Accounts of the Virginia Colonly, The First Decade: 1607–1617*. Ed. Edward Wright Haile. Champlain, VA: RoundHouse, 2001.

Hantman, Jeffrey L. "Between Powhatan and Quirank: Reconstructing Monacan Culture and History in the Context of Jamestown" in *American Anthropologist* 92, no. 3 (September 1990).

Hatch, Charles E. Jr. *The First Seventeen Years—Virginia, 1607–1624*. Charlottesville: University Press of Virginia, 1957.

Hening, William Waller. *The Statutes at Large; Being a Collection of All the Laws of Virginia, from the First Session of the Legislature, in the Year 1619, Vol. I*. New York: R. & W. & G. Bartow, 1823.

———. *The Statutes at Large; Being a Collection of All the Laws of Virginia, from the First Session of the Legislature, in the Year 1619, Vol. III*. Philadelphia: Thomas Desilver, 1823.

Hill, Samuel S. *Encyclopedia of Religion in the South*. Macon, GA: Mercer, 1984.

Jamestown Foundation, The. *Story of John Rolfe, Who Saved a Colony and Planted the Seeds of a Nation*. Published to commemorate the 350th anniversary of John Rolfe's first harvest, 1957.

Josephy Jr., Alvin M. *500 Nations*. New York: Knopf, 1994.

Kingsbury, Susan Myra, ed. *The Records of the Virginia Company of London, Vol. I*. Washington: Government Printing Office, 1906–1935.

Lewis, Clifford M., and Albert J. Loomie. *The Spanish Jesuit Mission in Virginia 1570–1572*. Chapel Hill: Published for the Virginia Historical Society by the University of North Carolina Press, 1953.

Pearce, Roy Harvey. *The Savages of America: A Study of the Indian and the Idea of Civilization*. Baltimore: Johns Hopkins Press, 1965.

Percy, George. *Observations Gathered out of "A Discourse of the Plantation of the Southern Colony in Virginia by the English, 1606."* Ed. David B. Quinn. Charlottesville: University Press of Virginia, 1967.

Purchase, Samuel. "An Interview in London" in *Jamestown Narratives: Eyewitness Accounts of the Virginia Colony, the First Decade: 1607–1617*. Ed. Edward Wright Haile. Champlain, VA: RoundHouse, 2001.

Rasmussen, William M. S., and Robert S. Tilton. *Pocahontas: Her Life and Legend*. Richmond: Virginia Historical Society, 1994.

Robinson, W. Stitt Jr. *Mother Earth: Land Grants in Virginia, 1607–1699*. Baltimore:

Clearfield, 1957.

Rolfe, John. Letter to Sir Thomas Dale, Virginia, 1614, in *Jamestown Narratives: Eyewitness Accounts of the Virginia Colony, The First Decade: 1607–1617*. Ed. Edward Wright Haile. Champlain, VA: RoundHouse, 2001. Handwritten copy made by Conway Robinson from a Dutch copy of the original in the Bodleian Library in Oxford, England. Photocopy made at The Virginia Historical Society, Richmond, Virginia, 2002.

———. "A True Relation of the State of Virginia" in *Jamestown Narratives: Eyewitness Accounts of the Virginia Colony, The First Decade: 1607–1617*. Ed. Edward Wright Haile. Champlain, VA: RoundHouse, 2001.

Rountree, Helen C. *Pocahontas's People: The Powhatan Indians of Virginia through Four Centuries*. Norman: University of Oklahoma Press, 1990.

———. *The Powhatan Indians of Virginia: Their Traditional Culture*. Norman: University of Oklahoma Press, 1989.

———. *Young Pocahontas in the Indian World*. Yorktown, VA: J & R Graphic Services, 1995.

Sams, Conway Whittle. *The Conquest of Virginia: The Third Attempt 1610–1624*. New York: G. P. Putnam's Sons, 1939.

Smith, John. "A True Relation" and "The Generall Historie of Virginia" in *The Complete Works of Captain John Smith (1580–1631) Vol. II*. Ed. Philip L. Barbour. Chapel Hill: University of North Carolina Press, 1986.

———. "A True Relation" and "The General History" in *Jamestown Narratives: Eyewitness Accounts of the Virginia Colony, the First Decade: 1607–1617*. Ed. Edward Wright Haile. Champlain, VA: RoundHouse, 2001.

Steinmetz, David C. *Calvin in Context*. New York: Oxford University Press, 1995.

Strachey, William. *The Historie of Travaile into Virginia Britinia (1612)*. London: The Hakluyt Society, 1849.

The New World, filmstrip. Written and directed by Terrence Malick, 2005.

Uttamatomakkin (Tomocomo). "An Interview in London" in *Jamestown Narratives: Eyewitness Accounts of the Virginia Colony, The First Decade: 1607–1617*. Ed. Edward Wright Haile. Champlain, VA: RoundHouse, 2001.

Waugaman, Sandra F., and Danielle Moretti-Langholtz, PhD. *We're Still Here: Contemporary Virginia Indians Tell Their Stories*. Richmond, Virginia: Palari Publishing, 2000.

Dr. Linwood "Little Bear" Custalow. Photograph by Angela L. Daniel "Silver Star"

Born on the Mattaponi reservation in West Point, the eldest son of Chief Daniel Webster "Little Eagle" and Mary "White Feather" Custalow, Dr. Linwood "Little Bear" Custalow grew up on the Mattaponi reservation, one of the oldest in the United States. Early in life, he was given the mission of learning the oral history of his tribe and of the Powhatan nation as passed down by his father, his grandfather, and those who came before. He left the reservation to pursue a higher education. Custalow, against many odds, became the first Virginian Indian to graduate from a college and a medical school in Virginia.

A member of the Phi Beta Kappa Honor Society, Custalow is a cofounder of the Association of American Indian Physicians, which today numbers more than 500.

He serves on the board of the Association for the Preservation of Virginia Antiquities. Recently retired from practicing medicine, Custalow lives in Williamsburg, Virginia, near the reservation. He is married and has four daughters.

Angela L. Daniel "Silver Star." Photograph
by Marjorie "Sunflower" Sargent

Angela L. Daniel "Silver Star's" roots trace back to an illiterate
grandfather and a grandfather who was a sharecropper. Daniel has a deep, long-standing interest in helping to put aside the
myths and misunderstandings surrounding the history of Virginia
Indians. Her own roots trace back to Indian ancestry, most likely
Cherokee. The late Chief Daniel Webster "Little Eagle" Custalow
honored Daniel by giving her the name "Silver Star." He encour-
aged her to learn and pass on the oral history of the Mattaponi.
Daniel received both a bachelor's and a master of arts from the
University of Virginia.

Today, she is working on her PhD in anthropology at the
College of William & Mary. She is the designated anthropologist
for the Mattaponi tribe. It has been said of Daniel, "She thinks like
an Indian; therefore, she is an Indian. She is one of us." Daniel's
life goal is to learn and preserve the oral history of the Powhatan
people so it can be passed down to future generations.

Look for Dr. Linwood "Little Bear" Custalow and Angela L. Daniel "Silver Star's" forthcoming publication, which provides an in-depth Mattaponi Powhatan historical account of the Mattaponi Powhatan oral tradition.

Edith "White Feather" Custalow Kuhns with her grandson Justin Kyle Whitman. The Mattaponi River is in the background. Photograph by Angela L. Daniel "Silver Star"

murder of, 51, 89
Pocahontas's marriage to, 43,
47, 80

L

Love marriages, 6
Luis, Don
boarding of Spanish ship by, 16
possibility of, as Wahunsenaca,
17
returning home of, 16–17

M

Marriage
alliance, 5–6, 8
love, 6
of Pocahontas to John Rolfe,
61–67, 70, 71, 74, 76, 79,
80, 86, 94
of Pocahontas to Kocoum, 43,
47, 80, 89
between Wahunsenaca and
Pocahontas (mother of Pocahontas), 6
Massacre of 1622, 33n
Matoaka, 6–7
Mattachanna (sister of Pocahontas),
7–8, 41–42
accompaniment of Pocahontas to
England and, 75, 90–91
in England, 81
reporting of poisoning of Pocahontas by, 83
reports back to Wahunsenaca
by, 81
return from England, 83
sending of, to be with Pocahontas, 62
Mattaponi tribe, 1, 6–7, 8, 14
Mattaponi village, life of Pocahontas
in, 7
McGowan, Rachel "Talking Moon," **2**

N

Native people, effect of disease on,
15, 17
Newport, Christopher, 21
Newton, Wayne, as descendant of
Little Kocoum, 90

O

Opechancanough (Wahunsenaca's
brother), 14–15, 93
negotiations for Pocahontas after
kidnapping of, 57–58
1622 attack on English, 93
Smith's claims concerning, 31, 33
turning over position of paramount chief to, 87
Opitchapam (Wahunsenaca's brother),
attendance at wedding of Pocahontas and Rolfe, 66
Oral history, concerns in writing, 1

P

Pamunkey River, 26
Pamunkey tribe, 1, 6–7, 14
Patawomeck tribe, 43
Patawomeck village, 47
Parahunt, 8
Pau-waus, 42
Pierce, Jane, marriage to John Rolfe, 91
Pocahontas
allegations of Smith concerning
saving of life by, 29–30
arrival of English colonists and,
11–12
baptism of, 58, 61, 64, 79
birth name of Matoaka, 6–7
birth of Thomas, 64, 65
brothers and sisters of, 7–8
burial of, in Gravesend, England,
83, 89
care of son, Little Kocoum, by
tribal women, 51
as child, 11
coming of age, 41–43

collection of information about
English colonists, 28
coming-of-age rituals in, 41–43
cultural standards of, 30–31, 55
curing of tobacco by *quiakros* in,
73–74
customs in, 5
differences between English society and, 35–36
division between childhood and
adulthood in, 11
English colonists taking of lands
from, 55, 76–77
English treatment of women and
children, 35–37, 40
hierarchical status in, 42
importance of *quiakros in*, 8,
12–13, 75
lack of attempt to rescue Pocahontas, 63–64
longevity as norm in, 86
outcasts in, 62–63
pau-waus in, 42–43
philosophy of acquiring more
through respectful and
peaceful means, 29–30
political structure in, 13
as priestly driven society, 35
quiakros within, 75
rape as not tolerated in, 35, 37,
62–63
Smith's betrayal of, 82
Smith's trade with, 14
stealing of wives and children in,
58–59
tribes in, 1, 12–13
welcoming of English colonists,
23–24
werowance in, 12, 13, 19–20
Powhatan territory
English settlements
from 1607 through 1616, **38**
by 1622, **39**
spies of English colonists in, 47–48

Powhatan tribe, 1, 8
Princess dance, 43

Q

Quiakros (priests)
desire for retaliation for Pocahontas's kidnapping, 55–56
efforts to prevent Pocahontas's
trip to England, 80–81
English colonists and, 13
growth of tobacco and, 71
importance of, within Powhatan
society, 8, 12–13, 75
jobs of, 13
kidnapping of Pocahontas and, 43
on poisoning of Pocahontas, 83
Powhatan society curing of
tobacco by, 73–74
Rolfe's challenge to establish good
relations with, 74
Smith and, 15
visits to Jamestown and, 24–25,
27, 28
warning that Pocahontas might
not return from England, 85
in Werowocomoco, 19–20
Quiyoughcosugh (one order of *quiakros*), 37

R

Rape as not tolerated in Powhatan
society, 35, 37, 62–63
Rasmussen, William M. S., 64
Rolfe, John, 91–92
arrival in Jamestown, 71
challenge to establish good relations with *quiakros*, 74
death of, 91
death of English wife, 73, 94
desire to return to Virginia, 83
dining of Pocahontas and, with
Argall on ship, 83
efforts to convert Pocahontas to
Christianity, 57